ABC delicious. More Please

120 all-new recipes for every season

valli little

8	**summer**
10	starters
32	mains
50	desserts
66	menus
68	**autumn**
70	starters
88	mains
114	desserts
126	menus
128	**winter**
130	starters
144	mains
168	desserts
186	menus
188	**spring**
190	starters
208	mains
230	desserts
244	menus
246	basics
250	index

Welcome

I'VE ALWAYS BEEN passionate about cooking with seasonal produce. Growing up in England, there was always great excitement at the arrival of the first Jersey Royal potatoes, spring lamb and sensational summer berries. And it's the wonderful produce we have here in Australia that's inspired me to create this new recipe collection.

I've noticed that a different kind of food culture is emerging in this country, where a new generation of cooks enjoys visiting farmers' markets, speaking directly to the producer of the meat, fruit or vegetables, then going home with their finds to create fabulous food for the family table.

That's what *delicious.* does best, and the idea behind *More Please* – exciting, creative recipes based on the seasons, that are all achievable for the home cook. You're sure to find inspiration for every occasion, whether it's simple family favourites such as my 'frypan pizza' or ice cream cupcakes; a themed dinner party such as hot and fiery hummus, Moroccan salmon and apple filo tarts; or a special occasion where you want to pull out all the stops with scallops with cauliflower skordalia, beef with porcini sauce and a luscious three-tier pavlova.

And why the title? Well, my family are my greatest critics when it comes to testing recipes, so the only dishes that have made it into this book are the ones where they held out their plates afterwards and said, "More, please!". I hope you'll all feel the same way.

Happy cooking,

Valli

2 x 750ml bottles dry white wine
½ cup (110g) caster sugar
2 ripe peaches, chopped
1 red apple, cut into thin wedges
1 orange, halved, thinly sliced
125g punnet raspberries
Handful of mint leaves
1 cup (250ml) vodka
   or peach schnapps
Soda water, to serve (optional)

Summer sangria

Combine the wine and sugar in a large jug or jar and stir until the sugar dissolves. Add the peach, apple, orange, raspberries, mint and vodka or schnapps, then stir gently to combine. Stand at room temperature for 2 hours to infuse.

Serve the sangria over ice, topped up with soda water if you prefer a long drink.

Serves 6-8.

700g small squid
300ml soda water
2 cups (300g) plain flour
¼ tsp cayenne pepper
Sunflower or grapeseed oil*,
   to deep-fry
Lemon wedges, to serve

Lime & ginger mayonnaise
1 egg
1 tsp Dijon mustard
Finely grated zest
   and juice of 1 lime
300ml sunflower or grapeseed oil
2 tsp grated fresh ginger

Fried squid with lime & ginger mayo

For the mayonnaise, place the egg, mustard and half the lime juice in a bowl. Whisk to combine, then gradually add the oil drop by drop, whisking constantly until all the oil is incorporated and you have a thick mayonnaise. Stir in ginger and lime zest. Add remaining lime juice to taste, then season with salt and refrigerate until needed.

Separate the squid tubes from the tentacles. Clean the tubes, then slice into 1cm rings. Remove and discard the beaks from the tentacles. Place the rings and tentacles in a bowl, then pour over the soda water and leave for 20 minutes to tenderise.

Combine the flour, cayenne and 1 teaspoon sea salt in a bowl. Drain the squid, then toss in the flour mixture to coat.

Half-fill a deep-fryer or large saucepan with oil and heat to 190°C. (A cube of bread will turn golden in 30 seconds when the oil is hot enough.) In batches, fry the squid for 1 minute or until just golden – any longer and it will become tough. Drain on paper towel, then sprinkle with salt and serve with the ginger mayonnaise and lemon wedges.

Serves 4.

* Grapeseed oil is a light, flavourless oil, available from supermarkets.

½ iceberg lettuce, leaves torn
1 avocado, sliced
1 mango, cut into 1cm cubes
12 large green prawns, peeled (tails intact)
2 tsp olive oil
1 tbs finely chopped chives

Cocktail sauce
⅓ cup (100g) mayonnaise
2 tbs tomato sauce (ketchup)
1 tbs thickened cream
1 tbs Worcestershire sauce
Juice of ½ lemon

Barbecued prawn cocktails

For the cocktail sauce, combine the mayonnaise, tomato sauce, cream, Worcestershire sauce and lemon juice in a small bowl. Season with sea salt and black pepper.

Divide the lettuce among 4 dishes, then add the avocado and mango and drizzle with a little cocktail sauce.

Heat a chargrill pan or barbecue to high. Brush the prawns with the oil and season well with sea salt and freshly ground black pepper. Chargrill the prawns for 1-2 minutes each side until lightly charred and cooked through.

Arrange 3 prawns on top of each salad. Drizzle with extra dressing and sprinkle with chopped chives. **Serves 4.**

Every time I go to Cumulus Inc. in Melbourne, I have to order Andrew McConnell's original version of this dish. I just love its simple, fresh flavours.

½ garlic clove, finely chopped
1 tbs soy sauce
Pinch of caster sugar
2 tbs olive oil
1 tsp balsamic vinegar
2 tsp finely grated lemon zest
250g sashimi-grade tuna*, cut into 2cm cubes
150g goat's curd*
Mustard cress* or snow pea shoots, to garnish

Pea salad
1 cup (120g) frozen peas, blanched
¼ cup (60ml) extra virgin olive oil
1 tbs lemon juice
1 eschalot, finely chopped
1 tbs mint leaves, finely chopped, plus extra leaves to garnish

Tuna tartare with crushed peas

Place the garlic, soy sauce, sugar, olive oil, balsamic vinegar and lemon zest in a bowl, stirring to dissolve the sugar. Add the tuna and stir gently to coat in the mixture, then cover and marinate in the fridge for 15 minutes.

Meanwhile, for the pea salad, place most of the peas in a mortar or a bowl, reserving some whole peas to garnish, and gently crush with the pestle or a potato masher. Add the oil, lemon juice, eschalot and chopped mint. Season well with sea salt and freshly ground black pepper, then stir to combine.

Remove the tuna from the fridge and bring to room temperature, then remove the tuna from the marinade.

Spread one-quarter of the goat's curd onto each serving plate. Arrange the pea salad over the goat's curd, then top with cubes of marinated tuna. Garnish with the reserved whole peas, extra mint and mustard cress. **Serves 4.**

* Sashimi-grade tuna is from fishmongers. Goat's curd is available from delis and gourmet food shops. Mustard cress is from selected greengrocers and supermarkets.

- 6 sheets frozen puff pastry, thawed
- 250g mascarpone cheese
- 2/3 cup (50g) finely grated parmesan
- 2 garlic cloves, finely chopped
- 2 tbs finely chopped basil, plus leaves to serve
- 6-8 brightly coloured heirloom tomatoes* (such as ox heart, yellow, kumato and green zebra) or vine-ripened tomatoes, halved, quartered or sliced
- Olive oil, to drizzle

Heirloom tomato tarte fine

Cut a 15cm circle from each pastry sheet, then place the circles on 2 baking paper-lined baking trays. Using a fork, prick the pastry all over, then chill for 30 minutes.

Preheat the oven to 180°C.

Top the pastry with another sheet of baking paper, then weigh the pastry down with a second tray. Bake for 8 minutes or until golden and crisp. Set aside to cool completely.

Meanwhile, combine the mascarpone, parmesan, garlic and chopped basil in a bowl and season well with sea salt and freshly ground black pepper. Spread the cheese mixture over the cooled pastry bases. Arrange whole basil leaves and tomato on top, season to taste, then drizzle with olive oil. Serve immediately. **Makes 6.**

* Heirloom tomatoes are from selected greengrocers and growers' markets.

1 telegraph cucumber
½ rockmelon
2 cups watercress sprigs
½ red onion, thinly sliced
2 tbs thick Greek-style yoghurt
175g soft blue cheese (such as gorgonzola dolce), sliced

Citrus dressing
Juice of 2 oranges (about ½ cup)
1 tsp caster sugar
1 tsp lime juice
2 tbs lemon juice
¼ cup (60ml) olive oil

Melon & blue cheese salad with citrus dressing

For the dressing, place the orange juice and sugar in a small saucepan over medium heat and simmer for 3-4 minutes until reduced by half (to about 3 tablespoons). Remove from the heat and add the lime juice and 1 tablespoon lemon juice. Slowly whisk in the olive oil, then season with salt and pepper. Set aside to cool completely.

Halve the cucumber, then thinly slice. Remove the skin and seeds from the rockmelon, then slice into wedges. Place the cucumber, melon, watercress and onion in a bowl and toss with half the dressing. Loosen yoghurt with the remaining 1 tablespoon lemon juice, then season to taste with salt and pepper.

Arrange the salad and gorgonzola on a platter or individual plates. Season, then drizzle with the remaining dressing and the lemon yoghurt. **Serves 4-6.**

1 egg
1/3 cup (50g) plain flour
1 garlic clove, finely chopped
Stalks of 4 coriander sprigs, roughly chopped
Kernels cut from 3 fresh corn cobs
200g fresh crabmeat*
2 spring onions, thinly sliced
Sunflower oil, to deep-fry
Lime wedges, to serve

Coriander dipping sauce
1/2 cup (110g) caster sugar
1/4 cup (60ml) rice vinegar
1 tbs fish sauce
1 tbs sweet chilli sauce
2 small red chillies, finely chopped
2 tbs coriander leaves, finely chopped

Crab & corn cakes with coriander dipping sauce

For the dipping sauce, place the sugar in a saucepan with the rice wine vinegar and 1/4 cup (60ml) water, then stir over low heat until the sugar dissolves. Cool slightly, then add the fish sauce, sweet chilli sauce, fresh chilli and chopped coriander leaves. Set aside the dipping sauce until needed.

Place the egg, flour, garlic, coriander stalks and one-third of the corn in a food processor and process to a rough paste. Add crabmeat and spring onion, then pulse briefly to just combine. Transfer to a bowl, then mix with the remaining corn kernels and season well with salt and pepper.

Half-fill a deep-fryer or large saucepan with oil and heat to 190°C (a cube of bread will turn golden in 30 seconds when the oil is hot enough). Working in batches, carefully drop a heaped tablespoon of batter into the oil for each fritter. Fry, turning, for 1-2 minutes until golden and crisp. Remove using a slotted spoon and drain on paper towel. Repeat to make 12 fritters in total. Serve immediately with the coriander dipping sauce and lime wedges. **Makes 12.**

* Fresh crabmeat is available from fishmongers.

Surprise! This looks just like a normal caprese salad, but our mozzarella look-alike is actually silken tofu.

¼ cup (60ml) light olive oil
2 tbs rice vinegar
1 tbs soy sauce
2 tsp caster sugar
½ tsp sesame oil

300g packet silken firm tofu
4 vine-ripened tomatoes, sliced
2 tsp toasted sesame seeds
Thai basil leaves*, to garnish

Asian-style caprese salad

Combine olive oil, vinegar, soy, sugar and sesame oil in a small bowl, stirring to dissolve the sugar. To replicate the look of bocconcini or mozzarella slices, slice the block of tofu into 4 slices and use a 4cm pastry cutter to cut 2 rounds from each slice, discarding any excess (you could also simply cube the tofu to minimise any wastage).

Arrange the tomatoes and tofu on each serving plate. Drizzle with the dressing and scatter with sesame seeds and Thai basil. **Serves 4.**

* Thai basil leaves are available from Asian food shops and selected greengrocers.

500g smoked salmon slices
500g soft cream cheese
2 tbs milk
2 tbs finely chopped chives
2 tsp capers, rinsed, chopped
Grated zest of 1 lemon, plus 2 tsp lemon juice, and lemon wedges to serve
Micro herbs, to garnish
Green salad, to serve

Crepes (makes about 25)
1 cup (150g) plain flour
1¼ cups (310ml) milk
2 eggs
40g unsalted butter, melted, plus extra to brush
Olive oil spray

Smoked salmon crepe cake

Grease and line a 20cm springform cake pan with plastic wrap, leaving plenty overhanging the sides.

For the crepes, place the flour, milk, eggs and butter in a food processor, season with salt and pepper, then process until smooth. Strain into a jug, then stand at room temperature for 30 minutes.

Meanwhile, roughly chop 150g smoked salmon and set aside. Place the remaining salmon in the cleaned food processor with the cream cheese, milk, chives, capers, lemon zest and juice. Process until smooth, then transfer to a bowl and fold through the chopped salmon.

Spray a 20cm crepe pan with olive oil spray and place over medium heat. Pour in enough crepe batter just to coat the base of the pan (about ¼ cup), returning any excess to the jug. Cook for 1-2 minutes each side until light golden, stacking crepes between sheets of baking paper as you go, to make about 25 crepes. Allow to cool.

To assemble the cake, layer the crepes in the prepared pan, spreading each with a thin layer of the filling and finishing with a crepe. Fold in the overhanging wrap to cover, then press down gently. Chill for at least 6 hours or overnight to set.

When ready to serve, transfer the cake to a serving platter, then cut into slices and garnish with the micro herbs. Serve with the lemon wedges and a green salad. **Serves 6-8.**

I learnt the tip about running the thyme under hot water to release the natural oils from Jamie Oliver – it works well with all coarse herbs and really boosts the flavour.

8 thyme sprigs
2 tbs olive oil, plus extra to serve
2 garlic cloves, finely chopped
500g piece beef eye fillet, trimmed
3 spring onions
Ice for an ice bath
250g punnet strawberries, quartered
1/4 cup (60ml) vincotto*, plus extra to drizzle
1/2 cup (40g) shaved parmesan
Micro herbs* or small purple basil leaves, to garnish

Beef carpaccio with strawberry vincotto

Run the thyme sprigs under hot water to release the natural oils. Remove the leaves from the stems and place the leaves in a dish with the olive oil, garlic, some salt and 1 teaspoon freshly ground black pepper. Add the beef and turn to coat in the mixture, then cover and stand at room temperature for 30 minutes to marinate.

Meanwhile, shred the spring onion into long, thin slices, then place in a bowl of iced water for 30 minutes to curl.

Heat a frypan over medium-high heat and sear the meat, turning, for 5-6 minutes until browned on all sides – be careful not overcook it as the centre should be rare. Remove from the frypan and allow to cool. Once the beef has cooled, enclose tightly in plastic wrap and place in the freezer for 15 minutes (this makes it easier to slice).

Toss the strawberries and vincotto in a bowl, season with salt and pepper, then set aside to macerate for 10 minutes.

Just before you are ready to serve, remove the beef from the freezer, slice 2mm thick and stand at room temperature for 10 minutes. Arrange on a large platter and scatter with the strawberries, spring onion and parmesan. Drizzle with extra vincotto and olive oil, season with salt and pepper, then garnish with micro herbs or basil. **Serves 6-8.**

* Vincotto is a condiment made from cooked grape must or figs, available from Italian and gourmet food shops; substitute balsamic vinegar. Micro herbs are available from growers' markets and selected greengrocers.

1 tbs sunflower oil
400g centre-cut sashimi-grade tuna*
1/4 cup (35g) white sesame seeds
1/4 cup (35g) black sesame seeds*
200g soba noodles*
1 cup shelled soy beans (edamame)*
1 Lebanese cucumber, cut into wedges
1 punnet snow pea sprouts, trimmed
1 avocado, sliced
4 spring onions, sliced on an angle
Pickled ginger*, to serve

Dressing
2 tsp caster sugar
1 tsp wasabi paste*
1/3 cup (80ml) ponzu (citrus soy)*
2 tbs mirin (Japanese rice wine)*
2 tsp fish sauce
Juice of 1 lime

Seared sesame tuna with soba noodles

Heat the oil in a frypan over high heat. Add the tuna and sear for 1 minute on each side – you want the tuna to remain rare on the inside. Allow to cool slightly.

Combine the sesame seeds on a clean chopping board and roll the cooled tuna in the seeds to completely coat. Enclose tuna tightly in plastic wrap, twisting ends to secure. Chill in the fridge for 30 minutes.

For the dressing, combine all the ingredients in a bowl and set aside.

Cook the soba noodles according to packet instructions, adding the soy beans for the final minute, then drain and refresh.

Meanwhile, remove the tuna from the fridge and slice 5mm thick.

Toss the noodles and soy beans with the cucumber, sprouts, avocado, spring onion and dressing. Divide among serving plates, then top with tuna slices and garnish with pickled ginger. **Serves 4-6.**

* Sashimi-grade tuna is available from fishmongers. All other ingredients are available from Asian food shops.

8 quail eggs*
2 green mangoes* or 1 green papaya*, shredded (a mandoline is ideal)
3 small red chillies, seeds removed, finely chopped
1 Asian red eschalot*, thinly sliced
1 cup each coriander, mint and Thai basil* leaves
2 x 175g hot-smoked salmon portions
50g salmon roe*
2 tbs fried Asian shallots*
2 tbs peanuts, roughly chopped

Dressing
3 large red chillies, seeds removed, finely chopped
2 small red chillies, seeds removed, finely chopped
2 garlic cloves, finely chopped
50g palm sugar*, grated
50ml fish sauce
100ml lime juice

Hot-smoked salmon salad with Thai flavours

For the dressing, shake all ingredients in a sealed jar until well combined. Taste and adjust balance of sweet, sour and salty if necessary.

Place the quail eggs in a small saucepan of cold water, bring to the boil, then cook for 3 minutes to soft-boil. Drain, refresh in cold water, then peel and halve. Set aside until needed.

Combine the mango or papaya, chilli, eschalot, coriander, mint and Thai basil in a bowl. Flake the salmon into rough pieces, discarding any skin and bones, then toss with the salad and enough dressing to moisten.

Divide the salad among serving bowls. Top with the quail eggs, chives and a spoonful of salmon roe. Garnish with fried Asian shallots and peanuts. **Serves 4.**

* Quail eggs, green mango, green papaya, Thai basil, fried shallots and palm sugar are from Asian food shops. Salmon roe is from delis and fishmongers.

- 3 large beetroots, scrubbed
- 1kg piece beef eye fillet (centre cut), trimmed
- 150ml extra virgin olive oil
- 2 red onions, cut into 5mm-thick rounds
- 2 garlic cloves, sliced
- 2 tbs chopped thyme leaves
- 100ml red wine vinegar
- 1 tbs wholegrain mustard
- 2 cups watercress sprigs

Goat's cheese dressing
- 150g soft goat's cheese
- 1/4 cup (60ml) buttermilk
- 2 tsp white wine vinegar
- 1 tsp chopped thyme leaves
- 1 tsp finely grated lemon zest, plus 1 tsp lemon juice
- 1 tbs chopped flat-leaf parsley

Beef fillet with beetroot and goat's cheese dressing

Preheat the oven to 200°C. Wrap each beetroot in foil, then place in a baking dish and bake for 1 hour or until tender. When cool enough to handle, peel, then slice 5mm thick.

Season beef, then heat 1 tablespoon oil in a large frypan over medium-high heat. Add the beef and cook, turning, for 3-4 minutes until browned all over.

Place the onion rounds and garlic in the base of a roasting pan, drizzle with a little oil, then season with salt and pepper. Sit the beef on top, sprinkle with thyme leaves and season with salt and pepper. Roast in the oven for 20 minutes for medium-rare (or until cooked to your liking), then transfer the beef to a plate, cover loosely with foil and leave for 10 minutes to rest. Use a spatula to carefully set aside the garlic and onion, keeping the rounds intact. Pour any pan juices into a bowl, then slowly whisk in the vinegar, mustard, remaining oil and any resting juices from the beef. Season with salt and pepper. Toss half the vinaigrette with the beetroot.

For the goat's cheese dressing, whisk everything together (or briefly process in a food processor) until combined and smooth, adding enough warm water (about 2-3 tablespoons) to make a loose dressing. Season to taste with salt and pepper. The dressing will keep, covered in the fridge, for 1 day.

To serve, slice the beef 2cm thick. Place a beetroot slice on each serving plate, then top with a slice of beef, some onion and watercress. Repeat layers, then spoon over remaining vinaigrette. Serve with the goat's cheese dressing to drizzle. **Serves 4-6.**

¼ cup (60ml) extra virgin olive oil
8 garlic cloves, bruised
1 cup flat-leaf parsley leaves
2 tsp grated lemon zest
450g fresh ricotta

½ cup (40g) grated parmesan,
    plus extra to sprinkle
1 baguette, split, or 2 large pizza bases
800g green prawns, peeled, halved
    if large (or 500g green prawn meat)

Garlic prawn pizza bread

Preheat the oven to 220°C and line a baking tray with baking paper.

Place the oil and garlic in a pan over low heat and warm gently for 2-3 minutes to infuse. Stand for 5 minutes. Remove garlic cloves (reserving oil), then place the cloves in a small processor with the parsley and lemon zest and whiz until combined. Set aside one-quarter of the mixture, then add the ricotta and parmesan to the remaining mixture and pulse to combine. Spread the ricotta mixture over the baguette or pizza bases.

Place the reserved garlic oil in a frypan over medium-high heat. Add the prawns and cook for 1 minute each side or until just cooked through. Remove from the heat, then add the reserved garlic and parsley mixture and gently toss to combine. Arrange the prawns over the baguette or pizza bases, then sprinkle with extra parmesan. Bake for 5-6 minutes until the cheese has melted. **Serves 4.**

Greek lamb meatball salad

⅓ cup (80ml) olive oil
1 onion, finely chopped
4 garlic cloves, finely chopped
1 tbs ground cumin
1 tsp paprika
500g lamb mince
1½ cups (105g) fresh breadcrumbs
1 egg, lightly beaten
1 cup (280g) thick Greek-style yoghurt
Juice of 1 lemon
2 tbs finely chopped mint leaves, plus extra leaves to garnish
2 baby cos, leaves separated
2 roasted capsicums (see Basics, p 246), cut into strips
1 small telegraph cucumber, halved lengthways, sliced
½ cup mixed marinated olives

Heat 1 tablespoon olive oil in a frypan over medium heat. Add the onion and cook, stirring, for 2-3 minutes until softened. Add the garlic, cumin and paprika and cook for 30 seconds or until fragrant, then transfer to a large bowl and allow to cool. Once cool, add the lamb, breadcrumbs and egg, season well, then combine. With damp hands, form the mixture into 20 walnut-sized balls. Chill in the fridge for 30 minutes.

Preheat the oven to 180°C.

Heat 1 tablespoon oil in a large frypan over medium heat. In batches, cook the meatballs, turning, for 3-4 minutes until browned all over. Place on a large baking tray and bake in the oven for 6-8 minutes until cooked through.

Place the yoghurt in a bowl with 2 tablespoons lemon juice and 1 tablespoon chopped mint. Season with salt and pepper, then stir to combine.

Arrange lettuce, capsicum, cucumber and olives on a large serving platter or in individual bowls. Lightly whisk the remaining 2 tablespoons olive oil with the remaining lemon juice and chopped mint. Season to taste, then drizzle the dressing over the salad. Scatter the meatballs on top, drizzle with the yoghurt and garnish with mint leaves.

Serves 4.

- ¼ cup (60ml) olive oil
- 1 red onion, finely chopped
- 3 garlic cloves, finely chopped
- 1 large rosemary sprig, leaves picked, finely chopped
- ½ tsp dried chilli flakes
- 400g cherry tomatoes, halved
- ¼ cup (60ml) red wine vinegar
- 2 tbs salted capers*, rinsed, drained
- ¾ cup (90g) green olives, pitted, chopped
- 1 tbs fresh oregano leaves, chopped
- 2 tbs chopped flat-leaf parsley
- 4 x 200g swordfish steaks
- Crispy potatoes and rocket, to serve (optional)

Chargrilled swordfish with tomatoes and olives

Heat 1 tablespoon olive oil in a frypan over medium heat. Add the onion and cook, stirring, for 2-3 minutes until softened. Add the garlic, rosemary and chilli and cook for 30 seconds until fragrant. Add the tomatoes and cook for 3 minutes or until they begin to soften. Add the vinegar and allow to bubble for 2-3 minutes until evaporated. Stir in the capers, olives and oregano and parsley, season to taste, then cook for a further 2-3 minutes until heated through. Set aside.

Meanwhile, heat a chargrill pan or barbecue to medium-high heat. Brush the swordfish with the remaining 2 tablespoons oil and season well with salt and pepper. In batches if necessary, cook the swordfish for 1 minute each side or until seared but still rare in the centre. Divide the swordfish and crispy potatoes among plates, spoon over the tomato mixture, then serve garnished with rocket. **Serves 4.**

* Salted capers are available from delis and gourmet food shops.

- 4 garlic cloves, finely chopped
- 2cm piece ginger, grated
- 1 tsp mild curry powder
- 100ml olive oil
- 4 French-trimmed pork cutlets
- 2 large yellow peaches
- 4 vine-ripened tomatoes
- 1 onion, finely chopped
- 2 tsp caster sugar
- 2 tbs red wine vinegar
- Coriander sprigs and green salad (optional), to serve

Pork cutlets with peach pan chutney

Combine the garlic, ginger, curry powder and ¼ cup (60ml) oil in a glass or ceramic dish. Season with salt and pepper, then add the pork cutlets and turn to coat in the mixture. Cover and marinate in the fridge for at least 10 minutes, or up to 2 hours.

Meanwhile, cut a cross in the base of the peaches and tomatoes. Blanch in boiling water for 1 minute, then plunge into a bowl of iced water. When cool enough to handle, peel, remove and discard tomato seeds and peach stones. Chop the flesh and set aside.

Preheat the oven to 180°C.

Heat 1 tablespoon oil in a large frypan over medium-high heat. Add the pork cutlets and cook for 2 minutes each side or until lightly browned. Place on a baking tray and cook in the oven for 10 minutes or until cooked through.

Meanwhile, return the pan to medium-low heat and add 1 tablespoon oil. Add the onion and cook, stirring occasionally, for 2-3 minutes until softened. Add the peach and tomato and cook, stirring, for 4-5 minutes until they soften and start to break down. Stir in the sugar and vinegar, then simmer for 3-4 minutes until thickened and lightly caramelised. Serve the pork with the pan chutney, coriander and a green salad, if desired. **Serves 4.**

8 thin prosciutto slices
16 sage leaves
8 good-quality pork chipolatas or other thin pork sausages
2 tbs plain flour, seasoned
¼ cup (60ml) olive oil
30g unsalted butter
150ml dry white wine
8 dinner rolls
1 garlic clove, halved
Rocket leaves, to serve

Sausage saltimbocca

Lay the prosciutto slices on a clean chopping board. Place 1 fresh sage leaf at the end of each slice. Place a sausage at the other end, then roll up to enclose the sausage in the prosciutto (making sure the sage leaf is visible). Secure with a cocktail stick or toothpick. Repeat with the remaining sausages. Toss the sausages in the seasoned flour, shaking off any excess.

Heat the oil in a large frypan over medium-high heat. Add the remaining sage leaves and cook for 1 minute or until crisp, then remove and drain on paper towel.

Drain all but 1 tablespoon oil from the pan, then add 2 teaspoons butter and place over medium heat. Cook the sausages, turning, for 4-5 minutes until cooked through. Transfer to a plate and keep warm.

Add the wine to the pan and allow to bubble for 3-4 minutes until the sauce thickens slightly. Add the remaining 20g butter and swirl to form a sauce, then season.

Meanwhile, split the rolls in half and place under a hot grill until lightly toasted. Rub the bread with the cut-side of the garlic clove. Place rolls on serving plates, top with sausages and rocket, drizzle with the sauce and garnish with fried sage. **Serves 4.**

5 cardamom pods
1 tbs sunflower oil
1 garlic clove, finely chopped
2cm piece ginger, grated
1 tsp ground turmeric
1 tsp ground cumin
1 tsp ground fenugreek
2 tbs lemon juice
1/3 cup (95g) thick Greek-style yoghurt
4 chicken thigh fillets, trimmed, quartered
1 tbs finely chopped mint leaves, plus extra leaves to serve
4 pieces of mountain bread or lavash bread
Butter lettuce leaves, to serve

Chicken tikka with minted yoghurt

Lightly crush the cardamom pods to remove the seeds, discarding the green husk.

Heat the oil in a frypan over low heat. Add the garlic, ginger, turmeric, cumin, fenugreek and cardamom seeds and cook, stirring, for 1 minute until fragrant. Cool slightly, then transfer to a ceramic or glass dish. Stir in lemon juice and 2 tablespoons yoghurt, then season well with salt and pepper. Add the chicken and turn to coat in the mixture. Cover and marinate in the fridge for at least 4 hours, or overnight.

Heat a lightly oiled chargrill pan or barbecue on medium-high heat. In batches if necessary, cook the chicken for 4 minutes on each side or until cooked through.

Meanwhile, stir the chopped mint into the remaining 2 tablespoons yoghurt, then season to taste with salt and pepper.

Serve the chicken hot or cold, with the flatbreads, minted yoghurt, lettuce and extra mint leaves. **Serves 4.**

1 tbs grated ginger
2 garlic cloves, grated
2 tbs plum sauce*
1 tbs tomato sauce (ketchup)
1 tsp dried chilli flakes
1 tbs maple syrup

1 tbs treacle
2 tbs olive oil
1.5kg pork spare ribs (2 racks)
Lemon wedges, to serve
Coriander leaves, to garnish

Sticky pork ribs

Combine the ginger, garlic, plum sauce, tomato sauce, chilli flakes, maple syrup, treacle and olive oil in a large, deep-sided tray or dish. Add the pork ribs and baste thoroughly in the marinade. Cover with plastic wrap, then marinate in the fridge for 1 hour.

Preheat the oven to 190°C and line a large baking tray with baking paper.

Place the ribs on a baking tray, reserving any of the marinade. Bake in the oven for 30 minutes, then remove from the oven and baste with the reserved marinade. Return to the oven for a further 40 minutes or until the meat is tender and the marinade is sticky and caramelised. Serve with lemon wedges, garnished with coriander. **Serves 4.**

* Plum sauce is available from Asian food shops and selected supermarkets.

Peach Melba tart

1 qty sweet vanilla pastry (see Basics, p 246), or Careme sweet shortcrust pastry*
4 ripe peaches (preferably slipstone), halved, stones removed
200ml pure (thin) cream
1 vanilla bean, split, seeds scraped
2 eggs, plus 1 extra yolk
¼ cup (55g) caster sugar
2 x 125g punnets raspberries
Icing sugar, to dust
2 tbs flaked almonds, lightly toasted

Grease a 12cm x 35cm loose-bottomed tart pan. On a lightly floured surface, roll out the pastry to 3-5mm thick and use to line the pan, pressing gently into the base and sides. Trim to fit, then chill for 30 minutes.

Preheat the oven to 190°C. Line pastry with baking paper and fill with pastry weights or uncooked rice. Blind-bake for 10 minutes, then remove the paper and weights and bake for a further 5 minutes until pale golden and dry. Reduce the oven to 170°C.

Meanwhile, blanch the peach halves in a pan of boiling water for 1 minute. Allow to cool slightly, then peel and pat dry with paper towel.

Heat the cream and vanilla pod and seeds in a saucepan over medium heat until just below boiling point. Gently whisk the eggs, extra yolk and sugar together in a bowl, then whisk the warm cream into the egg mixture, discarding the vanilla pod.

Place the peach halves, cut-side down, in the pastry case. Scatter with half the raspberries, then pour over the cream mixture. Bake in the oven for 35-40 minutes until the custard is set. Cool slightly, then dust with icing sugar and serve scattered with the almonds and remaining raspberries. **Serves 6.**

* Available from delis and gourmet food shops, visit: caremepastry.com.

Three-tier brown sugar pavlova

Icing sugar, sifted, to dust
½ firmly packed cup (110g) brown sugar
1½ tbs cornflour
1½ cups (330g) caster sugar
6 eggwhites (at room temperature)
1½ tsp vanilla extract
2 tsp white vinegar
500g mixed fresh (or frozen, thawed) berries
300ml thickened cream
200ml sour cream

Preheat the oven to 120°C. Grease and line the base and sides of three 24cm cake pans. Grease again, then dust with a little icing sugar, shaking off any excess.

Place the brown sugar, cornflour and 1 cup (220g) caster sugar in a food processor and whiz until the mixture is combined and fine (without any lumps).

In the bowl of an electric mixer, whisk the eggwhites with a pinch of salt until soft peaks form. With the motor running, slowly add the sugar mixture a little at a time, whisking until stiff and glossy. Fold in the vanilla and vinegar. Divide the mixture among the pans, then transfer to the oven and bake for 1 hour. Leave to cool completely in the switched-off oven with the door ajar.

Meanwhile, place the remaining ½ cup (110g) caster sugar in a pan with ½ cup (125ml) water. Stir over low heat until the sugar dissolves, then simmer, without stirring, for 2-3 minutes until thickened slightly. Cool, then add the berries. Transfer half the berry mixture to a blender and puree until smooth, then combine with remaining berry mixture and chill until needed.

Using electric beaters, beat thickened cream and sour cream together until thick.

Run a knife around the rim of each cake pan, then carefully remove the cooled meringues and peel away the paper.

Just before serving, place 1 meringue on a cake stand, then spread with one-third of the cream mixture and scatter with one-third of the berries. Repeat with the remaining meringues, cream and berries, drizzle with any remaining syrup, then serve immediately. **Serves 6-8.**

2 mangoes
1/3 cup (80ml) Cointreau or Malibu
250g sponge cake
250g mango, passionfruit
  & pineapple jam*
5 kaffir lime leaves*
200g mascarpone cheese
2 tbs icing sugar
2 tbs toasted coconut flakes

Coconut custard
6 egg yolks
125g caster sugar
1/4 cup (35g) plain flour
400ml can coconut milk
1 vanilla bean, split, seeds scraped
300ml thickened cream

Mango & coconut trifle

For the coconut custard, using electric beaters, whisk the egg yolks and caster sugar until thick and pale. Sift in the flour and gently fold into the egg mixture. Place coconut milk and vanilla pod and seeds in a small pan over medium-high heat and bring to just below boiling point. Gradually pour coconut milk over the egg mixture, discarding vanilla pod, then stir to combine. Return to the pan and place over low heat, stirring, for 5 minutes or until the mixture coats the back of a spoon. Cover the surface closely with plastic wrap to prevent a skin forming and allow to cool completely. Using electric beaters, whip 200ml cream to soft peaks, reserving 100ml. Fold the whipped cream into the coconut milk mixture. Cover the surface closely with plastic wrap to prevent a skin forming, then chill the custard until needed.

Cut 6 wafer-thin slices of mango and set aside to garnish. Peel the remaining mango and cut into cubes, then sprinkle with 1 tablespoon Cointreau and stand for 15 minutes to macerate.

Break the sponge into small pieces and place in a bowl, then drizzle with remaining 1/4 cup (60ml) Cointreau. Warm the jam and 3-4 tablespoons water in a small pan over low heat, then pour over the cake and gently stir to combine. Layer the cake in 6 glasses or 1 large serving dish, then top with the macerated mango and custard. Chill.

Place remaining 100ml cream and 4 kaffir lime leaves in a pan and gently warm over medium-low heat. Set aside to cool. Once cool, strain, discarding leaves, then beat with mascarpone and icing sugar until soft peaks form. Spoon on top of the trifles.

Finely shred the remaining lime leaf. Garnish the trifles with reserved mango slices, coconut flakes and shredded lime leaf. **Serves 6.**

* Mango jam is from supermarkets. Kaffir lime leaves are from Asian food shops.

500g fresh or frozen (thawed) raspberries, plus extra to serve
1/3 cup (75g) caster sugar
1/2 tsp vanilla extract
1 tbs lemon juice
2 gold-strength gelatine leaves*
160g white chocolate, chopped
300ml thickened cream, plus whipped cream to serve
2 tbs icing sugar
White chocolate shards, to serve (see Basics, p 246)

Raspberry & white chocolate mousse

Puree the raspberries, caster sugar, vanilla and lemon juice in a food processor, then pass through a sieve into a large bowl, pushing down on the solids to extract as much juice as possible. Set aside the puree, reserving 1/3 cup (80ml) separately to serve.

Soak the gelatine leaves in cold water for 5 minutes to soften. Squeeze to remove excess liquid, then place the leaves in a bowl with 1/3 cup (80ml) boiling water and stir to dissolve. Add the gelatine mixture to the bowl of raspberry puree and stir to combine.

Melt the chocolate with 1/3 cup (80ml) cream in a heatproof bowl set over a pan of simmering water (don't let the bowl touch the water). Set aside to cool.

Whip the remaining cream to soft peaks, fold into the cooled chocolate mixture, then fold into the raspberry puree. Divide among 4-6 bowls or serving glasses, then cover and chill in the fridge for at least 4 hours or overnight until set.

To serve, dust mousse with icing sugar, drizzle with reserved raspberry puree and whipped cream, then serve with extra berries and white chocolate shards. **Serves 4-6.**

* Available from gourmet food shops and delis. Check packet for setting instructions.

½ cup (80g) whole almonds, sliced
300ml thickened cream
4 eggs, separated
85g icing sugar, sifted
¼ cup (60ml) amaretto liqueur*
½ cup (80g) blanched almonds, toasted, finely chopped
8 amaretti biscuits*, crushed

Caramel sauce
½ cup (125ml) thickened cream
½ firmly packed cup (110g) brown sugar
2 tbs unsalted butter
1 tsp vanilla extract

Almond parfait

Grease and line a 1-litre terrine or 21cm x 10cm loaf pan with plastic wrap, leaving plenty overhanging the sides. Scatter the sliced almonds over the base to cover.

Using electric beaters, beat the cream to soft peaks, then set aside.

In a separate bowl, combine the egg yolks and icing sugar and beat with electric beaters until thick and pale. In a clean, dry bowl, whisk the eggwhites and a pinch of salt with electric beaters until soft peaks form.

Add the amaretto, toasted almonds and crushed amaretti to the egg yolk mixture and stir until well combined. Using a metal spoon, gently fold the whipped cream and eggwhite into the mixture, keeping as much air in the mixture as possible. Pour into the prepared terrine, packing down well. Gently tap the terrine several times on the bench to remove any air bubbles. Cover with the overhanging plastic wrap and freeze for at least 4 hours or overnight until firm.

For the sauce, place all the ingredients in a small saucepan over low heat and stir until the sugar has dissolved. Simmer, stirring occasionally, for 5 minutes or until slightly thickened. Allow to cool, then chill until ready to serve. (If the sauce has solidified in the fridge, microwave for a few seconds.)

To serve, briefly dip the terrine in warm water, then turn out onto a platter. Remove plastic wrap, drizzle with caramel sauce, then slice and serve. **Serves 8.**

* Amaretto is a liqueur made from bitter almonds or apricot kernels, from bottle shops. Amaretti biscuits are Italian almond biscuits from delis and selected supermarkets.

10 lemons
1 cup (150g) icing sugar, sifted
1/3 cup (80ml) limoncello liqueur*

300ml thickened cream
1 cup (240g) creme fraiche*
Mint leaves, to garnish

Limoncello ice cream wedges

Finely grate the zest of 4 lemons, then squeeze the juice (you need 1/2 cup (125ml) juice). Place the lemon zest and juice in a food processor with the icing sugar and limoncello, then process until combined.

Beat the cream and creme fraiche with electric beaters until thick, then stir in the lemon mixture. Churn in an ice cream machine according to manufacturer's instructions. Alternatively, pour the mixture into a shallow container and freeze for 2-3 hours or until frozen at edges. Remove and beat with electric beaters. Return to the container and refreeze. Repeat 2 or 3 times.

If you'd like to serve the ice cream in lemon wedges, halve the remaining lemons, then scoop out and discard the flesh. Fill with the churned ice cream mixture, then freeze for a further 1-2 hours until firm. Halve again to form wedges, then serve garnished with mint. **Serves 6-8.**

* Limoncello is from bottle shops. Creme fraiche is from delis and selected supermarkets.

Hibiscus flowers and strawberries have a wonderful synergy, turning this simple dessert into something quite exotic.

1 cup (220g) caster sugar
1 vanilla bean, split, seeds scraped
250g jar hibiscus flowers in syrup*
2 x 250g punnets strawberries, hulled, halved if large

Yoghurt sorbet
1/2 cup (110g) caster sugar
500g thick Greek-style yoghurt
1/2 cup (125ml) milk

Hibiscus strawberries with yoghurt sorbet

For the sorbet, place the sugar in a pan with 1/2 cup (125ml) water and stir over low heat until the sugar dissolves. Allow to cool slightly, then chill for 1 hour. Once it's completely cold, whisk in the yoghurt and milk, then churn in an ice cream machine according to the manufacturer's instructions. Alternatively, pour the mixture into a shallow container and freeze for 2 hours or until frozen at edges. Remove and beat with electric beaters. Return to the container and refreeze. Repeat 2 or 3 times.

To make the hibiscus strawberries, place sugar, vanilla bean and seeds in a pan with 1 cup (250ml) water and stir over low heat until the sugar dissolves. Simmer over medium-low heat for 10 minutes or until slightly reduced. Allow to cool, then stir in the flowers and syrup. Add the strawberries and leave to infuse for 30 minutes before serving in 6 glasses or small bowls, topped with a small scoop of the sorbet. **Serves 6.**

* Hibiscus flowers in syrup are from gourmet food shops (we used Essence of Wild Hibiscus from Nicholson Fine Foods, visit: nicholsonfinefoods.com.au).

- 2/3 cup (60g) desiccated coconut
- 1 cup (220g) caster sugar
- 1/2 tsp coconut extract* or vanilla extract
- 1 cup (250ml) sweetened condensed milk
- 1L (4 cups) coconut milk
- 300ml thickened cream
- 150g coconut ice confectionery*, broken into pieces
- Thinly sliced seasonal fruit (such as plums or peaches), to garnish

'Coconut ice' ice-creams

Place the desiccated coconut, caster sugar, coconut extract and condensed milk in a blender, then blend until combined. Transfer to a bowl and stir in the coconut milk. Using electric beaters, beat the cream to soft peaks, then fold into the coconut mixture. Churn in an ice cream machine according to manufacturer's instructions. Alternatively, pour the mixture into a shallow container and freeze for 2-3 hours until frozen at the edges. Remove from the freezer and beat with electric beaters, then refreeze. Repeat this process 2 or 3 times.

While the mixture is still soft, divide among eight 1/2 cup (125ml) dariole moulds or cups, then freeze until firm.

Meanwhile, place the coconut ice in a food processor and process to fine crumbs. Spread the coconut ice on a plate.

Run a warm knife around the edge of each mould, then turn out and roll in the coconut ice. Refreeze until needed, or serve immediately with sliced fruit. **Makes 8.**

* Coconut extract is available from delis and gourmet food shops. Coconut ice is from sweet shops, or use extra desiccated coconut and a few drops of pink food colouring.

Light Asian

24
Asian-style caprese salad

+

30
Seared sesame tuna with soba noodles

+

62
Hibiscus strawberries with yoghurt sorbet

Impress your friends

14
Barbecued prawn cocktails

+

34
Beef fillet with beetroot and goat's cheese dressing

+

50
Peach Melba tart

Teen party

- 36 Garlic prawn pizza bread
- 48 Sticky pork ribs
- 56 Raspberry & white chocolate mousse

Relaxed lunch

- 10 Summer sangria
- 42 Pork cutlets with peach pan chutney
- 60 Limoncello ice cream wedges

1L cider
½ cup (125ml) Calvados* or brandy
2 cinnamon quills
12 cloves
½ cup (175g) honey
3cm piece ginger, sliced
6-8 dried apple slices*
1 orange, sliced
1 lemon, sliced

Mulled cider

Place all ingredients in a large saucepan and warm gently over medium-low heat for 5-6 minutes. Allow to cool slightly, then divide among glasses and serve immediately.
Serves 6-8.
* Calvados is apple brandy, available from bottle shops. Dried apple slices are from selected greengrocers and gourmet food shops (we used Whisk & Pin).

Pimientos de Padron are green peppers that originate from Padron in northwest Spain. Watch out, though – one in every 10 of these delicious peppers are red-hot. I love serving them with drinks and watching my guests play Russian roulette!

30-40 pimientos de Padron*
½ cup (125ml) extra virgin olive oil

Chargrilled bread, to serve

Pimientos de Padron

Wash the pimientos and pat dry. Heat the olive oil in a large frypan over medium heat. Add the pimientos and cook, turning, for 5-6 minutes until the skins blister and the peppers start to wilt. Sprinkle with sea salt, then serve warm with drinks, chargrilled bread and other tapas dishes, such as marinated anchovies and pan-fried chorizo, if desired. **Serves 6.**

* You can order them from Queensland's Midyim Eco, midyimeco.com.au.

For a wonderfully intense flavour, infuse the olive oil with chilli overnight.

1/2 cup (125ml) extra virgin olive oil,
    plus 1 tbs to pan-fry
1 tsp dried chilli flakes
2 x 440g cans chickpeas,
    rinsed, drained
3/4 cup (75g) toasted walnuts
2 garlic cloves
2 tsp ground cumin
Juice of 1 lemon
1 red onion, finely chopped
150g lamb mince
1 tsp sumac*
2 tbs chopped coriander,
    plus extra leaves to garnish
Seeds of 1/2 pomegranate* (optional)
Flatbreads, to serve

Hot and fiery hummus

The day before you want to make the hummus, place the oil and chilli in a small pan and cook gently over low heat for 2-3 minutes, then stand overnight to infuse.

The following day, set aside 1/3 cup chickpeas. Place the remainder in a food processor with the walnuts, garlic, 1 teaspoon cumin, half the lemon juice and half the chilli oil. Process until smooth, then season. Taste the hummus and adjust the balance with lemon juice; you may also need to add a little warm water to achieve a soft, smooth consistency. Set aside the hummus while you prepare the lamb.

Heat 1 tablespoon oil in a frypan over medium heat, then add the onion and cook, stirring, for 3-4 minutes until soft. Add the lamb and remaining garlic and cook, stirring, for 6-8 minutes until the lamb is brown. Add the sumac and remaining cumin, season well, then stir in the chopped coriander.

When ready to serve, spread the hummus on a plate, then scatter with the lamb, pomegranate seeds and the reserved chickpeas. Garnish with the coriander leaves, and serve with flatbreads. **Serves 4.**

* Sumac is a lemony Middle Eastern spice made from ground dried berries, available from supermarkets and Middle Eastern shops. Pomegranates are available in season from greengrocers.

1 kumara (about 330g)
1 large potato (about 250g)
1/2 small carrot (about 75g)
1 small parsnip (about 150g)
1/4 tsp ground nutmeg
2 tbs finely chopped thyme leaves
1 egg
20g unsalted butter

1 tbs olive oil
1/3 cup (80g) creme fraiche
   or sour cream
2 tbs grated lemon zest,
   plus extra to sprinkle
175g hot-smoked salmon portion*,
   flaked
2 tbs finely chopped chives

Autumn rosti with hot-smoked salmon

Peel all the vegetables and cut into 4cm pieces. Place in a saucepan of cold, salted water and bring to the boil. Blanch for 4 minutes until just tender, then drain and allow to cool. Coarsely grate all the vegetables into a large bowl, then add the nutmeg, thyme and egg, season well and stir to combine. Form into 12 patties, then chill for 15 minutes.

Place half the butter and 2 teaspoons oil in a frypan over medium heat. Add half the patties and cook for 1-2 minutes each side until golden and crisp. Keep warm in a low oven while you repeat with the remaining butter, oil and vegetable mixture.

Combine the creme fraiche with lemon zest and some salt and pepper.

To serve, divide the rosti among plates, top with a dollop of creme fraiche and some smoked salmon, then sprinkle with chives and extra lemon zest. **Makes 12.**

* Available from supermarkets and delis.

150g matured goat's cheese*
¼ cup (60ml) walnut oil*,
 plus extra to brush
½ cup (60g) crushed toasted walnuts
6 slices walnut bread*
⅓ cup (80ml) olive oil

1 tsp honey
2 tbs lemon juice
1 radicchio,
 outer leaves discarded
2 cups watercress sprigs
1 ripe pear (such as Williams)

Goat's cheese, pear & walnut salad

Brush the outer rind of the goat's cheese with a little walnut oil and roll in the crushed walnuts. Cut the goat's cheese into 4 rounds, then chill for 15 minutes.
   Remove the crusts from the walnut bread, then cut the bread into 2cm croutons. Heat the olive oil in a small frypan and fry the croutons for 1-2 minutes, turning, until crisp. Remove and drain on paper towel.
   Whisk the walnut oil, honey and lemon juice together in a bowl, then season well.
   Divide the radicchio and watercress among 4 serving plates. Slice the pear into the salads, then scatter with the croutons.
   Preheat the grill to high and line a baking sheet with baking paper. Place the cheese slices on the baking sheet, drizzle with a little walnut oil, then grill for 1-2 minutes until the top is golden and the cheese has started to melt. Carefully place a slice of cheese on each salad, then drizzle with the dressing and serve. **Serves 4.**
* Matured goat's cheese and walnut oil are available from delis and gourmet shops. Walnut bread is available from selected bakeries; substitute sourdough.

2 cups (500ml) pure (thin) cream
6 garlic cloves
20g unsalted butter
10 anchovy fillets, drained
1/2 cup (35g) fresh breadcrumbs
Extra virgin olive oil, to drizzle
Chargrilled ciabatta, to serve
Blanched baby vegetables
   (such as baby carrots,
   golden and red baby beetroots,
   baby zucchini and cauliflower
   florets), to dip

Bagna cauda with baby vegetables

Place the cream and garlic cloves in a small pan over medium heat. Bring to a simmer, then reduce heat to low and cook for 15-20 minutes until the cream has reduced by half. Allow to cool slightly.

Meanwhile, melt the butter in a separate pan over medium-low heat, add the anchovies and gently heat for 1-2 minutes, stirring, until the anchovies start to dissolve. Place the cream, garlic, anchovies, butter and breadcrumbs in a blender and blend until smooth.

Place the warm bagna cauda in a bowl. Drizzle with olive oil, season with freshly ground black pepper and serve with grilled ciabatta and baby vegetables. **Serves 6-8.**

This is a modern twist on the grilled ham and cheese sandwiches made famous by Harry's Bar in Venice, the same bar-restaurant that invented the bellini and carpaccio.

250g fontina cheese*, chopped
¼ cup (60ml) thickened cream
1 tbs Dijon mustard
2 tbs Worcestershire sauce
¼ tsp dried chilli flakes
1 egg yolk

12 sourdough slices
6 prosciutto slices
2 tbs olive oil
30g unsalted butter
Fried flat-leaf parsley sprigs
   (optional), to garnish

Harry's Bar sandwiches

Place the cheese in a bowl, then stand in a warm place for 30 minutes to soften.

Place the cheese and cream in a food processor and pulse to combine. Stir together the mustard, Worcestershire, chilli and egg yolk, then stir into the cheese mixture until smooth. Season to taste with salt and pepper.

Remove the crusts from the bread, then spread the slices with the cheese mixture. Top half the bread with the prosciutto, then sandwich with the remaining bread. Cut each sandwich into 3 neat fingers. (At this stage, I find it's best to enclose them tightly in plastic wrap and chill for at least 30 minutes – this helps to maintain their shape when you cook them.)

Heat the oil and butter in a frypan over medium heat. In batches, fry the sandwiches for 1-2 minutes each side until golden. Serve scattered with sea salt and fried parsley sprigs, if desired. **Makes 18.**

* Fontina is an Italian cheese available from delis. Substitute another melting cheese.

350g cauliflower
300ml extra virgin olive oil, plus extra to drizzle
200g Dutch cream potatoes
2 cups (500ml) milk
6 garlic cloves
Grated zest of ½ lemon, plus 2 tbs lemon juice

12 scallops without roe
1 cup micro herbs* or coriander leaves

Curry dressing
150ml extra virgin olive oil
2 eschalots, finely chopped
2 tsp korma curry paste
50ml lemon juice

Scallops with cauliflower skordalia and curry dressing

For the dressing, heat 1 tablespoon oil in a small frypan over medium heat. Add the eschalot and cook, stirring, for 1-2 minutes until softened. Add curry paste, stir for a few seconds until fragrant, then place in a small processor and process with ¼ cup (60ml) olive oil (or stir together in a bowl). Transfer to a bowl, stir in remaining oil and lemon juice, then season to taste. For a smooth dressing, pass through a sieve, pressing down on solids. This dressing can be made up to 1 day in advance.

Preheat oven to 180°C. Break cauliflower into small florets. Toss half the florets in 1 tablespoon oil and season to taste. Spread on a baking tray and roast for 20 minutes.

Meanwhile, cut potatoes into pieces the same size as the cauliflower florets, then place in a pan with the milk, garlic and remaining florets. Simmer over medium-low heat for 8-10 minutes until tender, then drain, reserving liquid. Pass potato and cauliflower through a ricer or mouli into a bowl. Stir in lemon zest and juice, remaining olive oil and enough cooking liquid to make a smooth puree. Season skordalia and keep warm.

Season the scallops and drizzle with oil. Heat a frypan or chargrill pan over medium heat. In batches, cook the scallops for 30 seconds each side until golden but still slightly translucent in the centre.

Spread some of the skordalia on each plate, top with the scallops, then scatter with the roast cauliflower, sprinkle with micro herbs and drizzle with the curry oil. **Serves 4.**
* Micro herbs are from select greengrocers and farmers' markets.

This delicious soup is so easy to make. The puris, which come from my friend, English food writer Debbie Major, are a perfect accompaniment.

2 tbs olive oil
2 onions, finely chopped
450g carrots, cut into 2cm cubes
2 tsp grated ginger
1 tbs korma curry paste
1L (4 cups) chicken or vegetable stock
200ml coconut milk, plus extra to drizzle
Juice of 1 large lime
400g can cannellini beans, rinsed, drained
Toasted cumin seeds, to sprinkle

Cumin puris
100g wholemeal flour
100g plain flour, plus extra to dust
2 tbs sunflower oil, plus extra to shallow-fry
1½ tsp cumin seeds

Spicy bean soup with cumin puris

For the puris, sift the flours and a pinch of fine salt into a bowl, then rub in oil until mixture resembles breadcrumbs. Stir in the cumin seeds, then gradually stir in 150ml water to make a soft, slightly sticky dough. Turn out onto a lightly floured surface and knead for 5 minutes until smooth. Form the dough into a ball, lightly coat with oil, then place in a bowl. Cover with plastic wrap and stand at room temperature for 15 minutes. Divide the dough into 12 balls and dust heavily with flour. Roll each ball out to a 13cm disc. Pour 1cm of sunflower oil into a deep frypan over high heat and heat to 180°C or until a cube of bread turns a golden brown in 30 seconds. One at a time, shallow-fry the puris for 45 seconds each side until puffed and golden, adding more oil if needed. Drain on paper towel. Keep warm in a low oven while you make the soup.

Meanwhile, heat the oil in a large pan over medium-low heat. Add the onion and cook, stirring, for 2-3 minutes until softened but not coloured. Add the carrot and ginger and cook for a further minute. Stir in the curry paste and cook for 30 seconds until fragrant. Add the stock and bring to the boil, then reduce heat to medium-low and simmer for 8-10 minutes until the carrot is tender. Add the coconut milk, lime juice and beans and allow to simmer for a further 5 minutes. Blend with a hand blender (or cool slightly, then blend in batches in a blender) until smooth. Gently reheat over low heat. Divide the soup among bowls, drizzle with extra coconut milk, sprinkle with cumin seeds, then serve with the cumin puris. **Serves 4-6.**

1 tbs olive oil, plus extra to drizzle
1 onion, finely chopped
3 garlic cloves, finely chopped
1½ cups (105g) fresh breadcrumbs
50g Persian (marinated) feta*, crumbled
1 long red chilli, seeds removed, finely chopped
2 tbs finely chopped flat-leaf parsley,
2 tbs pine nuts, toasted
4 portobello or other large flat mushrooms
1 cup (250ml) good-quality pasta sauce
300g Roman beans* or green beans, trimmed

Baked mushrooms with pine nuts and feta

Preheat the oven to 180°C.

Heat the oil in a frypan over medium heat. Add the onion and cook, stirring, for 2-3 minutes until softened. Add the garlic and cook for 30 seconds, then transfer to a bowl with the breadcrumbs, feta, chilli, parsley and pine nuts. Season well, then stir to combine. Place mushrooms on a baking tray, cup-side up, then fill with the breadcrumb mixture. Drizzle with a little extra oil and bake for 15 minutes or until the mushrooms are cooked and the filling is golden brown.

Meanwhile, blanch the beans in a saucepan of boiling salted water for 2-3 minutes until just tender. Drain, then refresh.

Place the passata in a frypan over medium-low heat and gently warm through. Toss the beans in the passata and serve with the mushrooms. **Serves 4.**

* Persian feta is available from delis and supermarkets. Roman beans are available from selected greengrocers.

- ¾ cup (185ml) rice vinegar
- ½ cup (110g) caster sugar
- 2 carrots
- ½ daikon* (about 200g)
- 2 long red chillies, seeds removed, finely chopped
- 1 lemongrass stem (pale part only), finely chopped
- 2 garlic cloves, finely chopped
- ¼ cup (60ml) sunflower oil
- 450g pork fillet
- 2 tbs fish sauce
- 1 baguette
- 2 tsp soy sauce
- 3 tbs mayonnaise
- ¼ cup coriander leaves
- ¼ telegraph cucumber, thinly sliced

Vietnamese pork baguette

Place the vinegar, 4 tablespoons caster sugar and 100ml water in a small bowl. Add a pinch of sea salt, then stir until the sugar has dissolved. Cut the carrot and daikon into matchsticks (a mandoline is ideal), then add to the vinegar mixture and set aside for 2 hours to pickle. Drain.

In a large ceramic or glass dish, combine the chopped chilli, lemongrass, garlic and 2 tablespoons sunflower oil. Season the marinade with salt and pepper.

Slice the pork 1.5cm thick and lay between 2 pieces of plastic wrap or baking paper. Using a rolling pin, flatten out the pork slices until about 3mm thick, then place in the marinade, turning to coat. Cover and marinate in the fridge for at least 15 minutes.

Heat a wok or frypan over high heat and add the remaining 1 tablespoon sunflower oil. In batches, cook the pork for 1-2 minutes each side until browned and cooked through. Return all the pork to the pan, then add the fish sauce and the remaining sugar and cook for a few minutes until the pork is golden and caramelised.

Cut the baguette in half lengthways and brush the cut sides with soy sauce on one side and mayonnaise on the other. Fill the baguette with pork, cucumber, carrot, daikon and coriander leaves. Cut into quarters, tie with kitchen string, if desired, and serve immediately. **Serves 4.**

* Daikon is a large white radish, from greengrocers and Asian food shops.

Olive oil spray
24 egg wonton wrappers*
¾ cup (185ml) orange juice
¼ cup (60ml) Chinese black vinegar*
2 tbs soy sauce
2 tbs sesame oil
1 tbs honey
1 tbs mirin (Japanese rice wine)*
1 tbs finely grated ginger
1 garlic clove, finely chopped
1 long red chilli, seeds removed, finely chopped
½ barbecue chicken, meat shredded
1 cup (80g) finely shredded wombok (Chinese cabbage)*
1 small carrot, cut into matchsticks
½ cup coriander, finely chopped
½ cup mint, finely chopped, plus extra leaves to garnish
¼ cup roasted peanuts, chopped

Spicy chicken salad in wonton cups

Preheat the oven to 180°C. Spray a 6-hole Texas (185ml) muffin pan with oil.

On a work surface, lay out 4 wonton wrappers in a square with the edges slightly overlapping. Brush the overlapping sides with water so the wrappers stick together to form a large square. Repeat with remaining wonton wrappers. Use these large squares to line the muffin holes – you will have to fold some of the edges down to form a cup shape. Spray with more oil and place in the oven for 7 minutes or until crisp and golden, watching carefully as they brown easily.

Meanwhile, place orange juice in a small pan over medium-high heat. Bring to the boil, then simmer for 3 minutes or until reduced by half. Allow to cool, then combine with vinegar, soy, sesame oil, honey, mirin, ginger, garlic and chilli.

Toss the chicken, wombok, carrot, coriander, mint and peanuts with the dressing. Pile into wonton cups, garnish with mint leaves and serve immediately. **Makes 6.**

* Available from Asian food shops and selected supermarkets.

Pumpkin & leek tart with pan-fried mushrooms

700g pumpkin, peeled, cut into 3cm-thick slices
1 tbs olive oil
1 qty savoury shortcrust pastry (see Basics, p 246)
40g unsalted butter
2 leeks (white part only), thinly sliced
3 garlic cloves, roughly chopped
¼ cup (60ml) dry white wine
300ml pure (thin) cream
2 eggs, plus 1 egg yolk
2 tsp chopped thyme leaves
2 tbs chopped flat-leaf parsley
1 cup (125g) grated gruyere cheese
Pinch of freshly grated nutmeg

Pan-fried mushrooms
40g unsalted butter
2 garlic cloves, finely chopped
400g mixed wild mushrooms* (such as pine, chestnut and shiitake)
¼ cup (60ml) dry white wine
2 tbs chopped flat-leaf parsley

Preheat the oven to 180°C. Line a baking tray with baking paper and grease a 26cm loose-bottomed tart pan. Place pumpkin on the tray, drizzle with olive oil and season with salt and pepper. Cover the tray with foil and roast in the oven for 25 minutes or until pumpkin is soft. Place pumpkin in a sieve over a bowl and allow to drain for 30 minutes.

Meanwhile, roll out pastry on a lightly floured surface to 5mm thick, then use to line the tart pan. Chill for 15 minutes, then line with baking paper and fill with pastry weights or uncooked rice. Blind-bake in oven for 10 minutes, then remove paper and weights and cook for a further 5 minutes or until golden and dry.

Meanwhile, melt butter in a large frypan over medium-low heat. Add the leek and garlic and cook, stirring, for 3-4 minutes until leek softens. Add the wine and reduce for 2-3 minutes until most of the liquid has evaporated, then cool slightly. Place the pumpkin, leek mixture, cream, eggs, yolk, thyme and parsley in a food processor and process until smooth. Stir in the cheese and nutmeg, then season well. Pour pumpkin mixture into tart shell, then bake for 40 minutes until firm and golden.

Meanwhile for the mushrooms, heat butter in a pan over medium heat. Add garlic and mushrooms and cook, stirring, for 2-3 minutes until mushrooms have wilted. Add wine and allow to bubble for 2-3 minutes until wine has evaporated and mushrooms are tender. Toss with parsley, then scatter over tart and serve. **Serves 4-6.**

* From selected greengrocers and growers' markets.

This is a really easy way to make an indulgent cheese sauce for pasta – you simply melt Taleggio and cream together over low heat.

400g large pasta shells (conchiglioni)*
2 tbs olive oil, plus extra to toss
1 3/4 cups (210g) peas
2 large zucchini
100g pancetta or bacon, finely chopped
1 garlic clove, grated
Grated zest of 1 lemon
500g Taleggio cheese*, chopped
300ml thickened cream
Pinch of nutmeg
1/4 cup (20g) grated parmesan

Taleggio, pea & pancetta pasta bake

Preheat the oven to 180°C and grease a large baking dish.

Cook the pasta shells in boiling salted water according to packet instructions until just tender. Drain, then refresh and toss in a little olive oil.

Meanwhile, cook peas in boiling water for 2-3 minutes until tender. Drain and refresh. Coarsely grate the zucchini. Place the zucchini in a colander, sprinkle with salt, then set aside for 10 minutes. Rinse and pat dry.

Heat the oil in a frypan over medium heat. Add the pancetta and cook, stirring, for 2-3 minutes until starting to crisp. Add the garlic, zucchini and lemon zest, then cook for a further 2 minutes. Season. Cool slightly, then place in a food processor with the peas and pulse to a coarse paste. Alternatively, roughly mash with a fork. Fill the pasta shells with the pea mixture, then arrange in the baking dish.

Place Taleggio and cream in a heatproof bowl set over a pan of simmering water, stirring occasionally, until the cheese has melted and the sauce is smooth. Season with nutmeg, salt and pepper. Pour the sauce over the pasta shells and sprinkle with parmesan. Bake in the oven for 20 minutes until golden and bubbling. **Serves 6-8.**

* Taleggio is an Italian washed-rind cheese from delis and cheese shops.

2 large strips of pared orange rind
1/3 cup (80ml) rice vinegar
1/2 cup (110g) caster sugar
1/4 cup (60ml) soy sauce
1/3 cup (80ml) beef stock or water
2 tsp Sichuan peppercorns*
1 tsp cornflour
400g rump steak, trimmed
2 tbs sunflower oil

2 carrots, cut into matchsticks
2cm piece ginger,
    cut into thin matchsticks
2 garlic cloves, thinly sliced
1 tsp dried chilli flakes
1 red capsicum, very thinly sliced
6 spring onions,
    thinly sliced lengthways
Steamed rice, to serve

Crisp stir-fried beef with orange

Preheat the oven to 150°C. Place the orange peel on a baking tray and bake in the oven for 30 minutes or until dry.

Combine the vinegar, sugar, soy sauce and stock in a small bowl, then set aside.

Meanwhile, heat a small frypan over medium heat and dry-fry the peppercorns for 30 seconds or until fragrant. Place in a mortar with the orange peel and crush to a powder. Combine powder with cornflour and 1/2 teaspoon salt. Slice the beef 1cm thick, then cut into 1cm strips. Toss to coat in the spice mixture. Set aside for 15 minutes.

Heat the sunflower oil in a wok over high heat. In 2-3 batches, stir-fry the beef for 30 seconds until crisp, making sure the oil is very hot again before cooking the next batch. Drain on paper towel. Reduce heat to medium-high, add the carrot, ginger, garlic, chilli and capsicum and stir-fry for 2-3 minutes, adding a little more oil if necessary. Return the beef to the wok with the sauce mixture, then stir-fry for 2 minutes or until well combined and heated through. Serve with steamed rice, garnished with the spring onion. **Serves 4-6.**

* Sichuan peppercorns are available from Asian food shops.

2 tbs olive oil
1 onion, finely chopped
2 garlic cloves, finely chopped
1 tsp ground cinnamon
1 tsp ground cumin
1/4 tsp ground turmeric
1/2 tsp sweet paprika
1/2 cup (125ml) chicken or vegetable stock
400g can chopped tomatoes
400g can chickpeas, rinsed, drained
400g small pasta shapes (such as orecchiette or penne)
1 cup each of mint, parsley and coriander leaves, plus extra to serve
100g pine nuts, toasted
Persian (marinated) feta*, to crumble
Sumac* and lemon wedges, to serve

Moroccan pasta

Heat the oil in a frypan over medium heat, then add the onion and garlic and cook, stirring, for 3-4 minutes until softened. Add the spices and cook for 30 seconds until fragrant, then add the tomatoes and stock or water, and simmer over medium-low heat for 10 minutes. Add the chickpeas and stir for 1-2 minutes until heated through.

Meanwhile, cook the pasta according to packet instructions. Drain, then add to the pan of sauce with the fresh herbs. Season well, then toss over low heat until combined. Place the pasta in a large serving bowl, then scatter with pine nuts, extra herbs, feta and sumac. Serve with lemon wedges to squeeze over. **Serves 4.**

* Persian feta and sumac, a lemony Middle Eastern spice made from ground dried berries, are available from supermarkets.

2 tbs olive oil, plus extra to deep-fry
2 tbs lemon juice
2 garlic cloves, finely chopped
2 tsp dried oregano
12 French-trimmed lamb cutlets
1 tbs cumin seeds
1 tsp smoked paprika (pimenton)*
1 kumara, peeled
1 parsnip, peeled
1 beetroot, peeled

Lamb cutlets with spiced vegetable chips

Combine olive oil, lemon juice, garlic and oregano in a large dish. Add lamb cutlets and turn to coat in the mixture, then cover and marinate in the fridge for 30 minutes.

Meanwhile, toast the cumin seeds in a dry frypan for 30 seconds or until fragrant. Place cumin in a mortar or spice grinder with the smoked paprika and $1/2$ teaspoon peppercorns, crush to a powder, then stir in 2 teaspoons sea salt.

Slice the kumara and parsnip about 1mm thick (a mandoline is ideal), then slice the beetroot last and keep separate to prevent it from staining the other vegetables.

Preheat a lightly oiled chargrill pan or barbecue on high heat. In batches, grill the lamb for 2-3 minutes each side until lightly charred but still pink in the middle, or to your liking. Cover with foil, then keep warm in a low oven.

Meanwhile, heat the oil in a deep-fryer or large saucepan to 190°C (a cube of bread will turn golden in 30 seconds when the oil is hot enough). Leaving the beetroot until last, cook the vegetables in batches for 1-2 minutes until crisp and golden. Drain on paper towel. Toss the vegetables in the seasoned salt and serve with the cutlets. **Serves 4-6.**
* Pimenton is available from gourmet food shops and delis.

1 tbs smoked paprika (pimenton)*
2 garlic cloves, finely grated
½ cup (125ml) olive oil
4 chicken breasts with skin on (wingbone attached – optional)*

400g can butter beans, rinsed, drained
2 fresh chorizos, chopped
200g roasted red capsicum*, chopped
2 tbs chopped flat-leaf parsley
Rocket leaves, to serve

Chicken with butter bean puree and crispy chorizo

Preheat the oven to 180°C.

Combine the paprika, garlic, 2 tablespoons olive oil and some salt and pepper in a large bowl. Add the chicken, turning to coat in the mixture, then cover and place in the fridge to marinate for 30 minutes.

Place butter beans in a pan with 100ml water and warm over medium-high heat for 2-3 minutes until warmed through. Cool slightly, then place in a food processor with 3 tablespoons olive oil and some salt and pepper, then puree until smooth. Set aside.

Heat the remaining oil in a frypan over medium-high heat. Cook the chicken for 2-3 minutes each side until golden, then place on a baking tray and roast in the oven for 8-10 minutes until cooked through. Cover loosely with foil and set aside.

Meanwhile, return the frypan to medum heat, add the chorizo and cook, stirring, for 3-4 minutes until crisp. Add the capsicum, parsley and any resting juices from the chicken and toss until heated through. If necessary, gently reheat the butter bean puree over low heat. Divide the butter bean puree among plates, top with the chicken, then scatter with the chorizo mixture and serve garnished with rocket. **Serves 4.**

* Pimenton and roast capsicum are from delis; or see Basics, p 246, to roast your own capsicum. Chicken breasts with skin are from poultry shops and selected butchers.

25g dried porcini mushrooms*
2 garlic cloves, crushed
2 tsp chopped thyme leaves
1/4 cup (60ml) extra virgin olive oil
4 x 200g eye fillet steaks
40g unsalted butter
400g mixed mushrooms (such as Swiss brown and chestnut), sliced if large
1/3 cup (80ml) dry Marsala*

1 cup (250ml) beef consomme*
150g creme fraiche or light sour cream
2 tbs chopped flat-leaf parsley

Garlic mash
1/2 cup (125ml) milk
80g unsalted butter
2 garlic cloves
1kg sebago potatoes, peeled, chopped

Steak with wild mushroom sauce

Soak the porcini in 1/3 cup (80ml) boiling water for 30 minutes to soften.

Meanwhile, combine the garlic, thyme, 2 tablespoons oil and some salt and pepper in a dish. Add the steaks, turning to coat in the mixture, then stand the steaks at room temperature to marinate while you make the mash.

For the mash, heat milk, butter and garlic over low heat until butter is melted, then set aside to infuse. Cook potatoes in boiling water for 8-10 minutes until tender. Drain. Mash or pass through a ricer or mouli. Beat in milk until smooth. Season. Keep warm.

Meanwhile, melt the butter and remaining oil in a frypan over medium-high heat. Add mixed mushrooms and cook for 3-4 minutes until tender. Drain porcini, reserving soaking liquid, then chop any large pieces and add to the pan of mushrooms. Cook for 1 minute, then add Marsala and reserved liquid and cook for 3-4 minutes until reduced by half. Add consomme and continue to cook for 6-8 minutes until sauce is reduced by half again. Stir in creme fraiche, then simmer over low heat for 3-4 minutes. Season, then keep warm.

Heat a chargrill pan or barbecue on high heat. Cook the steaks for 2-3 minutes each side for medium-rare or until cooked to your liking. Rest steaks, loosely covered, for 5 minutes. Add any resting juices and 1 tablespoon parsley to the mushroom sauce and reheat gently. Spread some garlic mash on each plate, top with steaks and mushroom sauce, then sprinkle with remaining parsley and serve. **Serves 4.**

* Dried porcini are from gourmet food shops and greengrocers. Marsala is an Italian fortified wine, from bottle shops; I like to use Pellegrino Marsala. Beef consomme is available in tetra packs from supermarkets; substitute good-quality beef stock.

2 garlic cloves, grated
½ tsp ground turmeric
1 tbs grated ginger
⅓ cup (80ml) olive oil
1kg diced lamb shoulder
20g unsalted butter
2 onions, chopped
1 cinnamon quill
1½ tbs ras el hanout*
400g can chickpeas, rinsed, drained
400g can chopped tomatoes
2 cups (500ml) lamb or beef stock
1 tbs honey
150g dried apricots
2 tbs sesame seeds, toasted

Couscous
¼ cup (60ml) olive oil
1 onion, finely chopped
Grated zest of 1½ oranges
½ cup currants
2 tsp smoked paprika (pimenton)*
2 tsp ground cumin
1 cup (250ml) orange juice
50g unsalted butter
2 cups (400g) couscous
2 tbs chopped coriander (optional)

Lamb & apricot tagine

Combine the garlic, turmeric, ginger and 2 tablespoons oil in a bowl. Add the lamb, turning to coat in the mixture. Cover and place in the fridge to marinate for 1 hour.

Heat remaining 2 tablespoons oil in a flameproof casserole over medium-high heat, In batches, seal the lamb for 2-3 minutes, turning until browned on all sides. Set aside.

Melt butter in the same pan over medium-low heat. Add onion and cook, stirring occasionally, for 5 minutes or until softened. Add cinnamon and ras el hanout, then return lamb to pan and gently toss to coat in the spices. Add chickpeas, tomatoes, stock and honey – you should have just enough liquid to cover the lamb. Increase heat to medium-high, bring to a simmer, then reduce heat to low and simmer, partially covered, for 45 minutes. Uncover and simmer for 30 minutes, stirring occasionally, then add apricots and simmer for a further 10-15 minutes until lamb is tender and sauce is rich.

For couscous, heat oil in a pan over low heat. Add onion, zest, currants and spices. Cook, stirring occasionally, for 10 minutes or until onion is soft. In a separate pan, bring juice, butter and 1 cup (250ml) water to the boil, then slowly add couscous. Remove from heat and stand, covered, for 5 minutes. Fluff with a fork, then stir in onion mixture and coriander, if desired. Serve tagine, scattered with sesame, with the couscous. **Serves 4.**

* Ras el hanout (a Moroccan spice blend) is from Middle Eastern and gourmet shops.

1.5kg rack of pork
100ml olive oil, plus extra to fry
1 large red onion, cut into wedges
6-8 fresh figs, base scored
20 sage leaves

1 tbs plain flour
2 tsp Dijon mustard
1/3 cup (80ml) dry Marsala*
1 1/2 cups (375ml) chicken stock
1/2 cup fig jam*, plus extra to serve

Roast pork with Marsala & fig sauce

Preheat the oven to 240°C.

Score the pork rind at 2cm intervals, then rub with the 2 tablespoons oil and sprinkle with sea salt. Place on a rack in a large roasting pan and roast for 15 minutes. Reduce heat to 200°C, add the onion and cook for a further 1 hour or until skin is crisp and pork is cooked through, adding the figs for the final 5 minutes.

Meanwhile, heat the remaining 3 tablespoons oil in a small frypan over high heat. Add the sage leaves and fry for 1 minute until crisp, then remove with a slotted spoon and drain on paper towel.

Remove pork, figs and onion from the roasting pan and place on a platter to rest, covered, while you make the sauce. Drain all but 1 tablespoon of fat from the roasting pan, then place the pan over medium heat. Add the flour and stir until combined. Whisk in the mustard, then the Marsala and stock. Bring to a simmer over medium heat, then add the jam and stir until combined. Cook, stirring occasionally, for 5-6 minutes until thickened. (You can strain the sauce at this stage, but I like to leave it a little chunky.)

Carve the pork and serve with the onion, figs, fried sage leaves, fig sauce and extra fig jam, if desired. **Serves 6.**

* Marsala is an Italian fortified wine from bottle shops; I like to use Pellegrino Marsala. Fig jam is available from gourmet food shops.

4 x 120g skinless salmon fillets,
   cut into 2cm cubes
2 limes (skin on), cut into 2cm cubes
1 fennel bulb, very thinly sliced
   (a mandoline is ideal),
   plus fennel fronds to garnish
2 oranges, peeled, sliced into 5mm
   rounds, plus strips of zest to garnish
1 small red onion, thinly sliced

Dressing
1/2 cup (125ml) olive oil
2 tbs white wine vinegar
Juice of 1 large lime
2 tbs chopped flat-leaf parsley

Salmon skewers with fennel & orange salad

Soak 8 bamboo skewers in cold water for 30 minutes.

Preheat a chargrill pan or barbecue to medium-high.

For the dressing, place the ingredients in a screwtop jar with some salt and pepper, and shake to combine. Taste and adjust seasoning if necessary. Set aside.

Place the salmon in a bowl and pour over half the dressing, turning to coat in the mixture. Thread alternating pieces of salmon and lime onto the skewers, then grill or barbecue for 2-3 minutes, turning, until lightly charred and just cooked through.

Arrange the fennel, orange and onion in 4 bowls. Dress the salads with the remaining dressing, then top with the salmon skewers. Garnish with fennel fronds and orange zest, then serve. **Serves 4.**

200g dark chocolate, chopped
250g unsalted butter, chopped
1¾ firmly packed cups (385g) brown sugar
4 eggs
1⅓ cups (200g) plain flour
¼ tsp baking powder
⅓ cup (35g) good-quality cocoa powder
450g jar dulce de leche*

Dulce de leche brownies

Preheat the oven to 180°C. Grease a 22cm square cake pan and line with baking paper, leaving plenty overhanging the sides.

Place the chocolate and butter in a small saucepan over low heat and stir until melted and smooth. Transfer to a bowl and stir in the brown sugar and eggs. Sift in the flour, baking powder and cocoa powder and stir gently to combine. Pour half the mixture into the prepared pan.

Dollop 8 teaspoonfuls of dulce de leche over the batter in the pan. Use a wooden skewer to gently swirl the caramel over the chocolate (but don't cut through the mixture, as this will spoil the brownies). Spread the remaining batter over the top and repeat with another 8 teaspoonfuls of the dulce de leche.

Bake for 35-40 minutes or until set (the dulce de leche will still be molten). Remove from the oven and allow to cool slightly. Run a knife around the edge of the pan to loosen, then use the baking paper to ease the slice out of the pan. Cut into 12 squares and serve warm or cold with remaining dulce de leche to dollop. **Makes 12.**

* Ready-made dulce de leche (South American milk caramel) is available from gourmet food shops and delis (or see Basics, p 246).

These remind me of the little fromages blancs that you get in France. Slightly sweetened, they're perfect with fruit at any time of year.

200g cream cheese
1/4 cup (55g) caster sugar
2 cups (500ml) pure (thin) cream
1 vanilla bean, split,
  seeds scraped

Caramel oranges
4 oranges
1 1/2 cups (330g) caster sugar
3 star anise
2 cinnamon quills

Cremets with caramel oranges

Cut 6 squares of muslin, cheesecloth or plastic wrap, then use to line 6 teacups or 150ml dariole moulds, leaving plenty overhanging the sides.

Place the cheese and sugar in a bowl and beat with electric beaters until smooth. Slowly add cream, beating constantly, then stir in vanilla seeds to combine. Press the cream cheese mixture into the cups, then cover with the overhanging cloth or wrap. Chill for at least 2 hours or overnight until firm.

For the oranges, cut away all the skin and white pith from the fruit, then slice thinly into rounds. Arrange the orange slices in a heatproof dish in a single layer. Combine the sugar and 1 1/2 cups (375ml) water in a pan over low heat, stirring to dissolve the sugar. Add spices and bring to the boil over medium-high heat. Reduce heat to medium then simmer, without stirring, for 10-15 minutes until you have a golden caramel, brushing down the sides of the pan with a wet pastry brush to prevent crystals forming. Pour the hot caramel over the oranges and leave at room temperature for 1-2 hours – the caramel will start to break down into a delicious sauce with some crunchy shards of toffee.

To serve, dip the base of each mould in warm water and carefully turn out onto serving plates. Remove the muslin and serve with caramel oranges. **Serves 6.**

300g pkt Careme dark chocolate shortcrust pastry*
1 cup (250ml) thickened cream
60g unsalted butter, chopped
¼ cup (60ml) light corn syrup* or glucose syrup*
1 cup (220g) caster sugar
2⅓ cups (350g) hazelnuts, roasted, skins removed
50g dark chocolate

Chocolate hazelnut tart

Roll out the pastry to 5mm thick, then use to line a 28cm loose-bottomed tart pan. Chill for 30 minutes.

Preheat the oven to 180°C.

Line the pastry with baking paper, and weigh down with pastry weights or uncooked rice. Blind-bake for 10 minutes, then remove paper and weights and return to the oven for a further 5 minutes until dry. Leave to cool while you make the filling.

Place the cream and butter in a pan over medium heat and bring to just below boiling point. Remove from the heat and set aside.

Place the corn syrup and ⅓ cup (80ml) water in a separate pan, then sprinkle with the sugar. Place over medium heat and cook, stirring occasionally, until the sugar has dissolved and the liquid is clear. Increase the heat to high and cook, without stirring, until a golden honey colour. Remove from the heat, then carefully whisk the cream mixture into the toffee. Return the pan to low heat and stir to dissolve any hard bits of toffee. Add the nuts and cook for 1 minute. Pour the mixture into the tart shell and bake for 17-20 minutes until the tart filling is firm. Remove from the oven and allow to cool.

Just before serving, melt the chocolate in a heatproof bowl set over a pan of simmering water (don't let the bowl touch the water). Use a spoon to quickly drizzle the chocolate back and forth over the tart. Alternatively, place melted chocolate in a zip-lock bag, snip off one corner of the bag, then drizzle over the tart. **Serves 6-8.**
* Careme pastry is from gourmet food shops (for stockists, visit: caremepastry.com) or use chocolate pastry (see basics, p 246). Light corn syrup and glucose syrup are from the baking aisle in supermarkets.

Adding aromatic herbs, such as sage, bay leaves or thyme, to poached fruits adds another dimension to their flavour.

2 cups (500ml) pure (thin) cream
1/2 cup (125ml) milk
3 cinnamon quills
1/2 tsp ground cinnamon
1/4 cup (55g) caster sugar
2 gold-strength gelatine leaves*
2 tbs brandy

Slow-roasted pears
4 pears (such as Williams or beurre bosc)
6 sage leaves
1/2 firmly packed cup (110g) brown sugar

Cinnamon panna cotta with slow-roasted pears

Combine the cream, milk, cinnamon quills, ground cinnamon and caster sugar in a small pan over medium heat. Bring to a simmer, then remove from the heat and leave to infuse for 1 hour.

Soak the gelatine leaves in cold water for 5 minutes to soften. Reheat the cream mixture over low heat. Squeeze excess water from the gelatine, then add the leaves to the hot cream, stirring to dissolve. Stir in the brandy, then strain through a fine sieve into a jug. Pour mixture into six 1/2 cup (125ml) ramekins or dariole moulds and chill in the fridge for 4 hours or overnight.

Meanwhile, for the pears, preheat the oven to 160°C. Peel, halve and core the pears, leaving the stems intact. Place the sage leaves, brown sugar and 1/3 cup (80ml) water in a flameproof casserole and stir over low heat until sugar has dissolved. Add the pears and transfer to the oven. Cook for 3 hours until pears are very tender. Cool.

When ready to serve, run a knife around the edge of each mould to loosen, then invert the panna cottas onto plates. Divide the pears among plates, then drizzle with any remaining pear syrup and serve. **Makes 6.**

* Gelatine leaves are from gourmet food shops and selected delis. Always check the packet for setting instructions.

250g unsalted butter
250g good-quality dark chocolate
4 eggs, separated
½ cup (110g) caster sugar
½ firmly packed cup (110g) brown sugar
⅓ cup (50g) plain flour
50g almond meal

Yin-yang chocolate cake

Preheat the oven to 170°C and grease and line a 23cm springform cake pan.

Melt the butter and chocolate in a heatproof bowl set over a pan of gently simmering water (don't let the bowl touch the water). Cool slightly.

In a large bowl, whisk egg yolks, caster sugar and brown sugar with electric beaters until thick and pale. Stir in cooled chocolate mixture, then fold in flour and almond meal.

In a clean bowl, whisk the eggwhites with a pinch of salt until soft peaks form, then gently fold into the cake mixture, taking care to keep as much air in the mixture as possible. Pour into the prepared pan, then bake for 30 minutes. The cake will still be a little moist in the centre but will firm on cooling. Cool in the pan for 10 minutes, then transfer to a rack to cool completely.

To make the yin-yang template, cut a 23cm circle of baking paper, then draw an S-shape down the centre to create 2 large 'commas'. Using a 20 cent coin as a guide, draw a circle on one side. Cut out the comma and circle to create half a yin-yang symbol. Place the template on one side of the cake and dust generously with cocoa powder. Shake the template clean, then place on the opposite side and dust liberally with icing sugar. **Serves 6-8.**

½ cup (110g) caster sugar
1 vanilla bean, split, seeds scraped
5 egg yolks
600g creme fraiche or sour cream
2 pomegranates*
1 tbs pomegranate molasses*
2 tbs brown sugar

Vanilla-bean semifreddo with pomegranate splash

Line a 1-litre, 8cm x 22cm loaf pan with plastic wrap, leaving plenty overhanging the sides.

Place sugar and vanilla bean and seeds in a pan with ½ cup (125ml) water. Stir over low heat to dissolve the sugar, then simmer over medium-low heat for 5 minutes or until clear and syrupy.

Beat the egg yolks with electric beaters until pale. Slowly add the hot syrup, beating constantly, then continue to beat for 5 minutes until thick and pale. Fold in the creme fraiche, then pour into the lined pan, cover with overhanging plastic wrap and freeze for at least 6 hours, or overnight.

To make the pomegranate splash, cut the pomegranates in half, then hold upside-down over a bowl and tap the skin firmly with a rolling pin to remove the seeds. Discard any white pith. Combine pomegranate molasses, brown sugar and 2 tablespoons boiling water in a bowl, stirring until the sugar dissolves. Allow to cool, then stir in the pomegranate seeds.

To serve the semifreddo, dip the base of the loaf pan into warm water, then turn the semifreddo out onto a plate. Remove plastic wrap, then slice and serve with the pomegranate splash. **Serves 6-8.**

* Pomegranates are from selected greengrocers in season. Pomegranate molasses is from Middle Eastern grocers and gourmet food shops.

MENUS

TV dinner

 **82** Harry's Bar sandwiches

 **86** Spicy bean soup with cumin puris

 **114** Dulce de leche brownies

Easy vegetarian

 **80** Bagna cauda with baby vegetables

 **88** Baked mushrooms with pine nuts and feta

 **116** Cremets with caramel oranges

Middle Eastern

 **74** Hot and fiery hummus

+

 **108** Lamb & apricot tagine

+

 **124** Vanilla-bean semifreddo with pomegranate splash

Sunday best

 **78** Goat's cheese, pear & walnut salad

+

 **110** Roast pork with Marsala & fig sauce

+

 **118** Chocolate hazelnut tart

¼ cup (60ml) brandy
1 cup (150g) frozen berries
2 tbs Chambord (raspberry liqueur)

Whipped cream and toasted marshmallows (optional), to serve

Hot berry toddies

Heat the brandy and berries in a pan over low heat for 2-3 minutes, stirring, until warmed through and berries have broken down. Stir in the Chambord, then remove from the heat. Pour into serving glasses, then top with a dollop of whipped cream and serve with toasted marshmallows, if desired. **Makes 2.**

3 tomatoes
1 tbs olive oil
1 onion, chopped
1 leek (white part only), chopped
1 celery stalk, chopped
2 garlic cloves, chopped
1 strip pared lemon rind
Bouquet garni*
1.25L (5 cups) fish stock*
4 x 150g skinless blue-eye fillets, cut into 4cm pieces
2 x 400g cans butter beans, rinsed, drained
Aioli* and chopped tarragon or parsley, and crusty bread, to serve

fish broth with beans and aioli

Cut a cross in the base of each tomato. Place in boiling water for 30 seconds, then drain and plunge into a bowl of iced water for 1 minute. Once cool enough to handle, peel, then chop the tomatoes, discarding the seeds.

Heat the oil in a large pan over medium heat. Add the onion, leek, celery and garlic and cook, stirring, over low heat for 3-4 minutes until soft but not coloured. Add the chopped tomato, lemon rind, bouquet garni and stock. Bring to a simmer, then reduce heat to low and cook for 30 minutes or until reduced by half.

Strain the mixture, discarding solids, then return the broth to the pan. Add the fish and simmer for 5 minutes or until cooked through, then add the beans and warm through for a further minute.

Ladle the soup into shallow bowls, add a dollop of aioli, then scatter with tarragon or parsley leaves and serve with crusty bread. **Serves 4-6**

* A bouquet garni is a small bunch of herbs such as parsley, thyme and bay leaves tied with kitchen string. Fish stock is from fishmongers. Aioli is from delis and gourmet food shops; or see Basics, p 246.

Often served at ski resorts to combat the winter chill, this "cheat's" version of the French tartiflette makes for a filling winter supper.

2 large potatoes, peeled, cut into 2cm cubes
1 tbs olive oil
4 bacon rashers, chopped
1/3 cup (80ml) dry white wine
1 tsp chopped thyme leaves
1/3 cup (80g) creme fraiche or sour cream
4 slices sourdough bread
8 slices gruyere or cheddar cheese
Bitter salad leaves, to serve

Tartiflette on toast

Cook the potato in boiling salted water for 3 minutes or until just tender. Drain.
    Meanwhile, heat the oil in a frypan over medium heat. Add the bacon and cook, stirring, for 3-4 minutes until starting to crisp. Add the potato and cook, stirring, for 1-2 minutes until the potato starts to colour. Add the wine and allow to bubble for 2-3 minutes until it has evaporated, then stir in the thyme leaves and creme fraiche. Season the tartiflette with sea salt and freshly ground black pepper.
    Preheat the grill to high. Toast the bread on both sides, then top with the potato mixture and cheese. Grill for 1-2 minutes until the cheese is bubbling and melted. Season with freshly ground pepper. Serve with a salad of bitter leaves. **Serves 4.**

- 3 cups (750ml) good-quality chicken stock
- 3 cups (750ml) coconut milk
- 3cm piece ginger, peeled, cut into matchsticks
- 2 lemongrass stems, bruised
- 2 long red chillies, sliced
- 8 kaffir lime leaves*
- 175g mixed Asian mushrooms (such as shiitake, shimeji and enoki)*, trimmed
- 2 chicken breasts, thinly sliced
- 1/4 cup (60ml) fish sauce
- 1/3 cup (80ml) lime juice, plus lime wedges to serve
- 2 tsp brown sugar
- Coriander leaves, to garnish

Asian chicken & coconut soup

Place the chicken stock, coconut milk, ginger, lemongrass, chilli and 6 kaffir lime leaves in a saucepan. Bring to the boil, then reduce heat to medium-low and simmer for 5 minutes to infuse.

Add the mushrooms and chicken, then cook for a further 5 minutes until the chicken is cooked through and the mushrooms are tender. Add the fish sauce, lime juice and brown sugar, then adjust seasoning to taste.

Finely shred the remaining kaffir lime leaves. Divide the soup among bowls, then serve garnished with coriander and shredded kaffir lime leaf, with lime wedges to squeeze over. **Serve 4-6.**

* Available from Asian food shops and selected greengrocers.

1 tbs olive oil
4 onions, thinly sliced
2 tbs brown sugar
2 tbs balsamic vinegar
375g block puff pastry, thawed
4 thin bacon rashers
1 tbs thyme leaves
1 egg, lightly beaten
20g unsalted butter
4 spring onions, thinly sliced
100ml thickened cream
100g grated parmesan

Onion & bacon tart with parmesan cream

Preheat the oven to 200°C. Line a large baking tray with baking paper.

Heat the oil in a large frypan over medium-low heat. Add the onion and cook for 5-6 minutes, stirring occasionally, until softened. Add the sugar and balsamic and continue to cook for 4-5 minutes until dark and caramelised. Cool completely.

Roll out pastry to 2-3mm thick, then cut a 25cm circle. Score a 2cm border around the edge, then place the pastry on the prepared tray. Spread the caramelised onions over the pastry, taking care not to go over the border. Top with bacon, scatter with half the thyme, then brush the exposed edge with the egg. Bake in the oven for 20 minutes or until puffed and golden.

Meanwhile, to make the parmesan cream, melt the butter in a small saucepan over medium-low heat. Add spring onion and cook for 1-2 minutes until soft. Add cream and remaining thyme and bring to a simmer, then cook for 2-3 minutes until slightly reduced. Stir in the parmesan and season to taste. Cool slightly, then puree in a blender until smooth. (This can be made 2 days in advance, then gently reheated before serving.)

Drizzle the parmesan cream over the tart, then slice and serve. **Serves 4-6.**

Mussels in cider

30g unsalted butter
4 baby or 1 large leek (white part only), thinly sliced
2 garlic cloves, finely chopped
6 bacon rashers, chopped
400ml good-quality alcoholic cider
1kg mussels, scrubbed, debearded
100g creme fraiche or sour cream
2 tbs finely chopped flat-leaf parsley
Crusty bread, to serve

Melt the butter in a large pan over medium heat and add the leek, garlic and bacon. Cook for 5 minutes, stirring occasionally, until the leek has softened.

Add the cider and mussels and bring to a simmer. Cover with a lid and cook for 3-5 minutes until the mussels have opened. Remove and set mussels aside, then strain the cooking liquid. Return the liquid to the pan, then place over low heat and whisk in the creme fraiche or sour cream. Stir in the parsley, then season well with sea salt and freshly ground black pepper.

Return the mussels to the pan and gently warm through over low heat, then divide among bowls and serve with crusty bread. **Serves 4.**

4 ham hocks*
1 onion, finely chopped
1 carrot, finely chopped
1 cup (250ml) dry white wine
4 thyme sprigs
6 peppercorns
1 cup flat-leaf parsley, finely chopped
4 gold-strength gelatine leaves*
Baguette, cornichons and butter, to serve

Piccalilli
1/4 cup (55g) caster sugar
1/2 tsp ground turmeric
1/4 cup (60ml) white wine vinegar
300g small cauliflower florets
150g small green beans
1 red capsicum, thinly sliced
1 yellow capsicum, thinly sliced
1 onion, thinly sliced
1 tbs English mustard
1 long red chilli, seeds removed, sliced

Ham hock terrine with fresh piccalilli

Line a 1-litre terrine with plastic wrap, leaving plenty overhanging the sides.

Place ham hocks, onion, carrot, wine, thyme and pepper in a large pan. Cover with cold water and bring to the boil. Reduce heat to low and simmer for 3 hours, skimming occasionally, then remove from the heat and leave to cool. Once cool, remove ham hocks and reserve 1 cup (250ml) cooking stock. Flake meat from hocks, discarding skin and bones, then mix the meat with the parsley. Reheat reserved cooking stock over low heat.

Meanwhile, soak gelatine in cold water for 5 minutes to soften. Squeeze to remove excess liquid, then add leaves to the warmed stock and stir to dissolve.

Pack meat into terrine and cover with the liquid. Cover with overhanging plastic, then chill for 2 hours to set slightly. Top with a piece of cardboard cut to fit top of terrine, and weigh down with unopened cans. Chill for at least 8 hours, preferably overnight, until set.

For the piccalilli, place the sugar, turmeric and vinegar in a pan over low heat, stirring to dissolve sugar. Set aside. Blanch cauliflower in boiling, salted water for 2 minutes, then add beans and cook for a further minute. Drain, then refresh in cold water. Once cool, toss in a bowl with the vinegar mixture and the remaining ingredients. Chill for 2-3 hours or until ready to serve.

Remove the terrine from the mould, garnish with parsley sprigs, then slice and serve with the baguette, cornichons, butter and piccalilli. **Serves 4-6.**

* Ham hocks are from delis and butchers. Gelatine is from gourmet shops and delis.

Deconstructed Lasagne

Layers of herbed ricotta and flavoursome beef ragu make this a satisfying pasta when you don't have time to make a traditional lasagne.

2 tbs olive oil
2 onions, chopped
2 garlic cloves, chopped
1 tbs chopped rosemary
1/2 tsp dried chilli flakes
Grated zest of 1 lemon
1/4 cup salted capers, rinsed, chopped
4 tbs (1/3 cup) tomato paste
600g beef mince
2 tbs balsamic vinegar
1/2 cup pitted kalamata olives, chopped
1/2 cup flat-leaf parsley leaves, chopped, plus 2 tbs extra for the ricotta
2 x 400g cans chopped tomatoes
500g lasagnette pasta*
1 cup (240g) fresh ricotta
1/2 cup (40g) grated parmesan, plus extra to serve

Heat the oil in a pan over medium-low heat. Add the onion, garlic and rosemary and cook, stirring occasionally, for 2-3 minutes until softened. Add the chilli, lemon and capers and cook for a further minute, then add the tomato paste and cook, stirring, for 30 seconds. Add the beef and cook, breaking up with a wooden spoon, for 3-4 minutes until browned. Add the balsamic, olives, parsley and chopped tomatoes. Season with salt and pepper, bring to a simmer, then reduce heat to low and cook, stirring occasionally, for 30-40 minutes until thick and rich.

When the sauce is almost ready, cook the pasta in a large pan of boiling salted water according to packet instructions. Drain, then toss with the sauce.

Stir the extra parsley through the ricotta. Season, then place a dollop of ricotta in the base of 4-6 bowls. Top with pasta, sprinkle with parmesan, then add another dollop of ricotta and serve. **Serves 4-6.**

* Lasagnette is a long, wide, curly-edged pasta, from gourmet shops and delis. Substitute another long, wide pasta, such as pappardelle.

1 tbs olive oil
1 onion, finely chopped
500g beef mince
200g mushrooms, chopped
2 tbs tomato paste
2 tbs plain flour
1 tbs Worcestershire sauce
1 cup (250ml) beef consomme*
2 sheets frozen shortcrust pastry, thawed
2 sheets frozen puff pastry, thawed
1 egg, beaten
Tomato sauce (ketchup), to serve

Mushy peas
3/4 cups (185ml) chicken stock
1 1/4 cups (150g) frozen peas
5 mint leaves
1 tbs mascarpone or creme fraiche

Homestyle pies

Heat the oil in a large pan over medium heat. Add the onion and cook, stirring, for 3-4 minutes until soft. Add the mince and cook, stirring, for 4-5 minutes until browned. Add the mushrooms and tomato paste and cook, stirring, for a further 2-3 minutes, then stir in the flour, Worcestershire sauce and beef consomme. Bring to the boil, then reduce heat to medium-low and simmer for 10 minutes or until the mixture has thickened. Season with sea salt and freshly ground black pepper, then allow to cool.

Preheat the oven to 200°C.

Grease 8 individual pie dishes (about 11cm long). Cut each shortcrust pastry sheet into 4 equal pieces and use to line the pie dishes. Cut each puff pastry sheet into 4 equal pieces. Fill pies with the cooled meat mixture, then top with puff pastry lids, pressing the edges to seal. Trim off any excess pastry, then crimp the edges with a fork or your fingers. Use pastry trimmings to decorate the top of the pies, if desired. Brush the tops with beaten egg, then bake for 20 minutes or until golden.

Meanwhile, make the mushy peas. Place the stock in a pan and bring to the boil. Add the peas and cook for 2-3 minutes until tender. Add mint, then blend with a stick blender or use a potato masher to roughly mash. Season to taste with salt and pepper, then stir in the mascarpone or creme fraiche. Keep warm.

Serve the pies with mushy peas and, of course, tomato sauce. **Makes 8.**

* Beef consomme is available in tetra packs from supermarkets. Substitute good-quality beef stock.

- 3 large pontiac or desiree potatoes, peeled, cut into 2cm cubes
- 1/4 cup (60ml) sunflower oil
- 30 fresh curry leaves*
- 1 tsp cumin seeds
- 1/2 tsp coriander seeds
- 1/2 tsp ground turmeric
- 2 garlic cloves, sliced
- 1 long red chilli, seeds removed, sliced
- 3cm ginger, grated
- 3 tbs (1/4 cup) Indian curry paste
- 400ml coconut milk
- 2kg whole ocean trout or other whole fish, cleaned
- Plain yoghurt, steamed rice, mango chutney and naan bread*, to serve

Goan-style baked fish

Preheat the oven to 180°C. Line a roasting pan with baking paper.

Cook the potato in boiling salted water for 3-4 minutes until par-cooked. Drain.

Heat the sunflower oil in a frypan over medium-high heat. Add half the curry leaves and fry for 1 minute or until crisp, then remove with a slotted spoon and drain on paper towel.

Add cumin, coriander, turmeric, garlic, chilli, ginger and remaining curry leaves to the pan and cook, stirring, for 30 seconds or until fragrant. Add the potatoes and cook, stirring to coat in the spices, for 1-2 minutes until light golden, then stir in the curry paste and coconut milk. Season, then bring to the boil and cook for 3-4 minutes to allow the flavours to infuse.

Make 3 deep slashes in the flesh of the fish, then season well with salt. Place the fish in the lined roasting pan. Scatter the potatoes around the fish, then pour over the sauce. Bake for 25 minutes or until the fish is cooked through.

Carefully lift the fish and potatoes onto a platter, then pour over the curry sauce. Garnish with fried curry leaves and serve with yoghurt, steamed rice, mango chutney and naan bread. **Serves 6.**

* Fresh curry leaves are available from Asian food shops and selected greengrocers. Naan bread is available from Indian takeaway shops and supermarkets.

1kg boneless pork belly (skin on)
½ firmly packed cup (110g) brown sugar
⅓ cup (80ml) red wine vinegar
2 star anise
1 cup (250ml) chicken stock

Juice of 1 lime, plus wedges to serve
1 cup mint leaves
1 cup coriander leaves
1 cup Thai basil leaves*
3 spring onions, thinly sliced
1 long red chilli, seeds removed, thinly sliced

Pork belly with caramel dressing

Preheat the oven to 220°C.

Score the pork belly skin at 1cm intervals. Place the pork on a rack in a roasting pan, skin-side up. Rub 2 tablespoons salt into the skin, then pour in enough water to fill the pan to just under the rack. Roast for 30 minutes or until the skin is crispy, then reduce the oven to 180°C and roast for a further 1½ hours or until the meat is tender, topping up with water as necessary.

Meanwhile, place the brown sugar, vinegar and star anise in a pan over low heat, stirring to dissolve the sugar. Simmer for 5 minutes, then add the chicken stock and simmer for 5-6 minutes until reduced by half. Add the lime juice and continue to reduce for 3-4 minutes until syrupy.

Carve the pork into bite-sized cubes and arrange on a platter. Drizzle with the caramel dressing, then scatter with herbs, spring onion and chilli. Serve with lime wedges to squeeze over. **Serves 6.**

* From Asian food shops and selected greengrocers.

1 tbs olive oil, plus extra to serve
50g unsalted butter
1 small onion, finely chopped
1 celery stalk, chopped
6 slices white bread (200g), crusts removed, torn
1 tbs finely chopped sage
4 slices jamon* or prosciutto, roughly chopped
1 egg
½ cup (50g) grated manchego cheese*
1 large (about 1.8kg) free-range chicken
6 thin slices chorizo
300ml chicken consomme*
100g quince paste*
Patatas bravas, to serve (see Basics, p 246)

Spanish roast chicken with quince sauce

Preheat the oven to 200°C.

Heat the oil and butter in a pan over medium heat. Add the onion and celery and cook, stirring, for 2-3 minutes until soft. Cool slightly.

Meanwhile, place the bread in a food processor and pulse until finely chopped. Add the sage, jamon and onion mixture and pulse until coarsely chopped. Add the egg and cheese, season with salt and pepper, then pulse until combined. Cool completely.

Starting from the neck of the chicken, slide your fingers underneath the skin to loosen it from the breast, being careful not to tear the skin. Insert chorizo slices under the skin. Stuff the chicken cavity with the bread mixture, then tie the legs with kitchen string. Sit the chicken in a roasting pan, drizzle with olive oil, then season with salt and pepper. Bake the chicken for 1 hour 15 minutes or until the juices run clear when the thickest part of the thigh is pierced. Transfer the chicken to a plate and cover to keep warm.

Drain the excess fat from the roasting pan. Add the consomme and quince paste to the pan, then place over medium heat and whisk until the paste has dissolved and the sauce is heated through. Strain into a serving jug.

Slice chicken and serve with the sauce and patatas bravas. **Serves 4.**

* Jamon (cured ham), manchego (a hard sheep's-milk cheese) and quince paste are from Spanish food shops and delis. Chicken consomme is available in tetra packs from supermarkets; substitute good-quality chicken stock.

750ml bottle red wine
2 tbs olive oil
2 tbs plain flour, seasoned, to dust
6 beef cheeks*, trimmed
2 onions, chopped

4 garlic cloves, chopped
2L good-quality beef stock
2 bay leaves
Mashed potato and salsa verde (see Basics, p 246), to serve

Braised beef cheeks with salsa verde

Preheat the oven to 170°C.

Place the wine in a pan and simmer over medium heat for about 10 minutes or until reduced by half. Set aside.

Heat oil in a large flameproof casserole over medium-high heat. Dust the beef cheeks in seasoned flour. In batches, brown the beef cheeks for 2 minutes on each side until sealed, adding a little more oil if necessary. Remove and set aside.

Add the onion to the pan, reduce heat to medium and cook, stirring, for 5 minutes or until softened. Stir in the garlic, then return the beef cheeks to the pan. Add the reduced wine, beef stock and bay leaves. Season with salt and pepper. The meat should be completely covered with liquid, so top up with water if necessary. Cover and cook in the oven for 2½ hours or until the beef is meltingly tender. Remove the beef to a plate, then cover with foil to keep warm.

Place the casserole over medium-high heat and simmer for 5-10 minutes until the sauce thickens. Serve the beef with the sauce, with mashed potato and salsa verde.

Serves 6.

* Order beef cheeks from butchers.

4 good-quality fresh chorizo
or other spicy sausages
2 tbs olive oil
4 egg yolks
300ml pure (thin) cream

1/3 cup (25g) grated parmesan,
plus extra to serve
400g spaghetti or fettuccine
2 tbs chopped flat-leaf
parsley leaves

Chorizo carbonara

Remove the casings from the chorizo and roll the meat into bite-sized balls (you should get about 50).

Heat the oil in a frypan over medium heat. In 2-3 batches, cook the meatballs, turning, for 2-3 minutes until browned and cooked through. Drain on paper towel.

Beat the egg yolks, cream and parmesan together in a bowl. Season well with salt and pepper, then set aside.

Meanwhile, cook the pasta in boiling salted water according to packet instructions. Drain the pasta, then return to the hot pan. Add the chorizo and the cream mixture and toss well to coat (the residual heat will gently cook the egg). Add the parsley and toss to combine, then serve with extra parmesan. **Serves 4.**

Vegetable bhaji salad

- 250g besan (chickpea flour)*
- 1 tsp dried chilli flakes
- 1 tsp ground turmeric
- 1 tsp ground cumin
- 6 curry leaves*, finely shredded
- 200g sour cream or creme fraiche
- 1/3 cup (80ml) lemon juice
- 1 large carrot, cut into thin matchsticks
- 50g eggplant, cut into thin matchsticks
- 100g snow peas, cut into thin strips
- Sunflower oil, for deep-frying
- Mesclun (mixed baby salad leaves) or micro herbs*, to serve

Combine the besan, chilli, turmeric, cumin, 1/2 teaspoon salt and enough cold water to make a thickish batter, then stir through the curry leaves. Leave the batter to rest in the fridge for 15 minutes.

Combine the sour cream and lemon juice to make a loose dressing. Season with sea salt and freshly ground black pepper, then set aside.

Place carrot, eggplant and snow peas in a bowl, then toss with the batter.

Half-fill a deep-fryer or large saucepan with sunflower oil, then heat to 180°C (the oil is hot enough when a cube of bread turns golden in 30 seconds). Working in batches and using a heaped tablespoon of batter for each bhaji, drop spoonfuls into the oil and cook for 2 minutes each side, turning once, until golden and cooked through. Remove with a slotted spoon and drain on paper towel, then keep warm while you repeat with the remaining batter.

To serve, divide the salad leaves among 4 plates, top each with 2-3 bhaji, then sprinkle with salt and drizzle with the dressing. **Serves 4.**

* Besan flour and fresh curry leaves are from Asian food shops and selected greengrocers. Micro herbs are from selected greengrocers and growers' markets.

1 tbs peanut oil
8 spring onions (white part only), sliced on an angle
2 garlic cloves, finely chopped
1 lemongrass stem, halved
3 tbs red curry paste
1 Chinese barbecued duck*, chopped
400ml coconut milk
450g can pineapple pieces in natural juice, drained
3 kaffir lime leaves*
2 tsp brown sugar
2 tsp fish sauce
1/2 bunch coriander leaves, chopped, plus whole leaves to serve
Steamed rice and lime wedges, to serve

Duck & pineapple red curry

Heat oil in a wok over high heat. Add the spring onion, garlic, lemongrass and curry paste and stir-fry for 1 minute or until fragrant. Add the duck, coconut milk, pineapple, 2 kaffir lime leaves and chopped coriander. Bring to the boil, then reduce the heat to medium and simmer for 10 minutes or until the duck is warmed through and the sauce has reduced slightly. Add brown sugar and fish sauce to taste.

Finely shred the remaining kaffir lime leaf. Serve the curry, garnished with shredded kaffir lime and coriander leaves, with rice and lime wedges. **Serves 6-8.**

* Barbecued duck is from Chinese barbecue shops and restaurants; ask them to chop the duck for you. Kaffir lime leaves are from Asian food shops and greengrocers.

2 tbs olive oil
2 chorizo sausages, sliced
800g lean diced pork
2 onions, chopped
2 garlic cloves, chopped
1 tsp smoked paprika (pimenton)*
1 tbs plain flour
1/4 cup (60ml) sherry vinegar*
   or red wine vinegar
1 cup (250ml) dry sherry
1/2 cup (125ml) chicken stock
500ml tomato passata (sugo)*
3 thyme sprigs
2 bay leaves
1/2 cup small Spanish green olives
2 roasted red capsicums*, sliced
Torn flat-leaf parsley and
   chargrilled bread, to serve

Pork & olive stew

Preheat the oven to 170°C.

Heat 1 tablespoon oil in a large flameproof casserole over medium heat. Add the chorizo and cook for 2-3 minutes until starting to crisp. Remove and set aside. In batches, brown the pork, turning, for 3-4 minutes until sealed on all sides, adding a little more oil if necessary. Remove and set aside with the chorizo.

Add the onion and garlic and cook, stirring, for 2-3 minutes until softened. Stir In the paprika, then return the chorizo and pork to the pan. Stir in the flour, then add the vinegar, sherry, stock, passata, herbs and some salt and pepper, adding a little water to cover the meat if necessary. Bring to a simmer, then cover and transfer to the oven for 1 hour 15 minutes.

Add the olives and capsicum, then cover and return to the oven for a further 15 minutes or until the meat is tender and the sauce is reduced. Garnish with parsley and serve with chargrilled bread. **Serves 4.**

* Sherry vinegar is available from gourmet food shops and delis. Tomato passata and roasted capsicums are available from delis and selected supermarkets; or see Basics, p 246 to roast your own capsicum.

Asian poached beef on a string

Boeuf à la ficelle is a classic French dish. Adding Asian flavours, such as star anise, cinnamon and Sichuan pepper, makes for a lovely modern twist.

1½ tbs peanut oil
1kg piece of centre-cut beef fillet, trimmed
6 Asian (red) eschalots*, peeled
4cm piece ginger, thinly sliced
2 garlic cloves, bruised
2 star anise
1 cinnamon quill
1 tsp Sichuan peppercorns*
2 pieces dried orange peel*
2.5L beef stock
1 dried red chilli or ¼ tsp chilli flakes
2 tbs soy sauce
1 tsp sesame oil
Wasabi mash (see Basics, p 246) and steamed greens, to serve

Heat the oil in a large frypan over medium-high heat. Season the beef fillet, then brown for 4-5 minutes, turning, until sealed on all sides. Remove and set aside. Add eschalots to the pan and cook, turning, for 2-3 minutes until golden.

Place the eschalots, ginger, garlic, star anise, cinnamon, Sichuan pepper, orange peel, beef stock and chilli in large saucepan and bring to a gentle simmer over medium heat.

Tie the beef with kitchen string at 2cm intervals. Thread a large piece of string lengthways under the other pieces, then tie the ends of this string around a wooden spoon. Lower beef into the pan and rest the spoon across the top of the pan so the beef hangs down and is completely submerged in the stock. Reduce heat to medium-low, then cook for 20 minutes for medium-rare. Remove the beef and the eschalots from the pan. Set aside the beef to rest, covered, while you finish the sauce.

Strain 2 cups (500ml) of the liquid into a clean pan and simmer rapidly over medium-high heat for 10 minutes or until reduced by half. Add the soy sauce and sesame oil to the poaching liquid and season to taste.

Slice the beef and serve with the eschalots, wasabi mash and steamed greens, drizzled with the reduced sauce. **Serves 4-6.**

* Available from Asian food shops, greengrocers and selected supermarkets.

This is a lovely variation on a shepherd's pie that originated in South Africa.

1/4 cup (40g) sultanas
1/4 cup (60ml) brandy
2 tbs olive oil
2 onions, chopped
2 garlic cloves, finely chopped
1kg lamb mince
2 tbs mild curry powder

1/2 cup (125ml) tomato puree or passata
3 tbs apricot jam
4 eggs, plus 2 yolks
600ml thickened cream
1/2 tsp caster sugar
Green salad, to serve

Bobotie

Soak the sultanas in 2 tablespoons brandy for 2 hours.

Preheat the oven to 180°C.

Heat the oil in a pan over medium heat. Add the onion and cook, stirring, for 2-3 minutes until starting to soften. Add the garlic and cook for a further 1 minute until softened, then add the lamb and cook, stirring, for 6-8 minutes until browned. Add the curry powder, tomato puree and jam, then continue to cook over low heat for 3-4 minutes until the lamb is cooked through. Stir in the sultanas and soaking liquid, then spread into a 20cm x 30cm baking dish.

Beat the eggs, egg yolks and cream with some salt and pepper, then whisk in sugar and remaining 1 tablespoon brandy until combined. Strain through a sieve over the lamb. Place the baking dish in a roasting pan, then pour enough boiling water into the pan to come halfway up the sides of the baking dish. Bake in the oven for 40 minutes or until the topping is set and golden. Serve with a green salad. **Serves 6-8.**

Banana fruit loaf

Adding banana to this traditional tea cake keeps it extra moist. Just remember to soak the fruit a day ahead.

1 cup (160g) sultanas
3/4 cup (125g) raisins
125g currants
1 cup (250ml) cold, black tea
2 tbs brandy (optional)
2 ripe bananas, mashed
1 cup firmly packed (220g) brown sugar
1 cup (100g) chopped walnuts
1/4 cup (50g) glacé cherries, halved
1 egg, lightly beaten
2 tbs milk
2 tbs treacle*
2 2/3 cups (400g) self-raising flour, sifted
Butter, to serve

Place the sultanas, raisins and currants in a large bowl with the tea and brandy. Cover and leave to soak overnight.

The next day, preheat the oven to 180°C. Grease a 1-litre loaf pan and line the base and sides with baking paper.

Add the bananas, brown sugar, walnuts, cherries, egg, milk and treacle to the fruit. Sift in the flour, then fold everything together and spread in the prepared pan. Bake for 1 hour 15 minutes or until a skewer inserted in the centre comes out clean. (Cover loosely with foil if browning too quickly.)

Cool the cake in the pan for 10 minutes, then turn out onto a rack to cool completely. Slice and serve with butter, if desired. **Serves 6-8.**

* Available from the baking aisle in supermarkets.

1/3 cup (110g) strawberry jam
250g punnet strawberries,
	halved or quartered if large
1 1/2 cups (225g) self-raising flour
1 tsp baking powder
2 tbs caster sugar
50g unsalted butter, softened
1/3 cup (30g) desiccated coconut
50ml coconut cream

50ml milk,
	plus 1 tbs extra to brush
1 egg

Mascarpone cream
100g mascarpone cheese
1 1/2 tbs caster sugar
150ml coconut cream
150ml thickened cream

Coconut scones with strawberries and cream

To make the mascarpone cream, use electric beaters to mix the mascarpone in a bowl with the caster sugar and coconut cream until smooth. Whip the cream to soft peaks in a separate bowl, then gently fold through the mascarpone mixture. Cover and chill until needed.

Place jam and 2 tablespoons water in a pan over low heat, stirring until melted and combined. Add the berries and toss to coat. Set compote aside until needed.

Preheat the oven to 220°C and line a tray with baking paper. Sift the flour and baking powder into a bowl with a pinch of salt, then stir in the sugar. Rub in the butter using your fingertips, then stir in the desiccated coconut. Combine the coconut cream, milk and egg in a small bowl, then add to the dry ingredients, stirring with a knife. Bring the mixture into a ball using your hands (do not overmix), then turn onto a lightly floured workbench and form into a 5cm-thick, 12cm-diameter round. Use a 5cm cutter to cut 4 scones from the mixture, then bring together excess and make 2 more scones. Place on the prepared tray and brush with extra milk, then bake for 10-12 minutes until the scones have risen and the tops are golden.

Cool slightly, then split and serve with compote and mascarpone cream. **Makes 6.**

1 cup (250ml) milk
110g unsalted butter
2 tsp caster sugar
1 cup (150g) plain flour, sifted
5 large (70g) eggs, lightly beaten
200g mascarpone cheese
200g good-quality lemon curd*
Icing sugar, to dust

Lemon syrup
Zested rind of 3 lemons, plus 100ml juice
100g caster sugar

Lemon curd profiteroles

Preheat the oven to 220°C and line 2 large baking trays.

Place the milk in a saucepan with 1/2 cup (125ml) water, butter, sugar and a pinch of salt over medium heat. Bring to just below boiling point, then reduce the heat to low. Quickly add flour and beat with a wooden spoon until the mixture is well combined. Transfer to an electric mixture and add the eggs one at a time, beating well after each addition, until completely incorporated.

Spoon the batter into a piping bag fitted with a plain nozzle. In batches if necessary, pipe 3cm rounds of batter onto the trays, spaced 2cm apart. (If you don't have a piping bag, use 2 teaspoons to drop rounds onto the tray.) You should have about 50 profiteroles. Bake for 12 minutes, then turn the oven off and leave them to dry in the oven, with the door slightly ajar, for 15 minutes. Remove from the oven and leave to cool for 30 minutes, then repeat with the remaining batter if needed.

For the syrup, place lemon zest, juice and sugar in a pan over low heat. Stir to dissolve sugar, then simmer for 5 minutes, without stirring, until syrupy. Allow to cool completely. Meanwhile, beat mascarpone and lemon curd with electric beaters until thick. Chill.

To assemble, split each profiterole in half, pipe or spoon the lemon curd filling onto the profiterole bases, then return tops to cover. Pile onto a cake stand, then drizzle with the lemon syrup and dust with icing sugar just before serving. **Makes 50.**

* Lemon curd is available from delis and gourmet food shops; or see Basics, p 246, to make your own lemon curd.

- 4 green apples, peeled, cored, cut into 2cm pieces
- 1 tsp finely grated lemon zest, plus 2 tbs juice
- 1 vanilla bean, split, seeds scraped
- 1/2 cup (110g) caster sugar
- 1 tsp Fragrant Sweet Spices blend* or ground cinnamon
- 50g sultanas
- 1 tsp cornflour
- 4 sheets fresh filo pastry
- 80g unsalted butter, melted, cooled
- 2 tbs dried edible rose petals*
- Icing sugar, to dust

Rose custard
- 1 qty warm creme anglaise (see Basics, p 246)
- 2 tbs rosewater*
- Rose food colouring

Moroccan apple pies with rose custard

Preheat the oven to 200°C and grease 6 holes of a 12-hole medium muffin pan.

Place the apple, zest and juice, vanilla pod and seeds, sugar, spices, sultanas and 2 tablespoons water in a pan over low heat. Cover and cook for 6 minutes or until the apple is tender. Remove from the heat and allow to cool. When cool, mix the cornflour with 2 teaspoons hot water, then stir into the apple mixture.

Place filo sheets on top of each other, then slice into six 15cm squares to make 24 squares in total. Leaving the remaining pastry covered with a damp tea towel as you work, brush 4 squares with melted butter, then place in a muffin hole, positioning each layer at an angle to fill the hole entirely, leaving the pastry overhanging the edges. Repeat with remaining pastry to make 6 pie cases. Divide the filling among the pie cases, then fold in the sides to enclose. Brush the tops of the pies with a little more butter, then bake for 15-20 minutes until the pastry is golden.

Meanwhile, for the custard, mix the warm creme anglaise with rosewater and 1-2 drops of food colouring to taste.

Remove the pies from the oven, brush with the remaining butter and scatter with dried rose petals. Leave to cool slightly, then transfer to plates, dust with icing sugar and serve with the rose custard. **Makes 6.**

* Fragrant Sweet Spices and dried edible rose petals are from gourmet food shops and at herbies.com.au. Rosewater is from Middle Eastern and gourmet food shops.

125g unsalted butter, softened
125g caster sugar
1 tsp vanilla extract
4 eggs
1 2/3 cups (250g) self-raising flour, sifted

Finely grated zest of 1/2 lemon
1/3 cup (80ml) milk
1/2 cup (160g) blueberry jam
125g fresh or frozen blueberries
Pure (thin) cream, to serve

Steamed blueberry pudding

Preheat the oven to 180°C and grease a 1.25-litre (5-cup) pudding basin.

Beat the butter, sugar and vanilla in an electric mixer until pale and thick. Add the eggs one at a time, beating well after each addition. Fold in the flour and lemon zest, followed by the milk until combined (the mixture should be a soft dropping consistency).

Spread half each of the jam and berries in the base of the pudding basin, then pour in the batter. Layer a sheet of foil on top of a sheet of baking paper, then fold a pleat through the centre. Use to cover the pudding, then tie with string. Place in a roasting pan, then fill the pan with enough boiling water to come halfway up the sides of the basin. Cook in the oven for 1 hour 15 minutes or until a skewer inserted in the centre comes out clean. Stand for 5 minutes.

Meanwhile, warm the remaining jam with the berries over low heat for 2-3 minutes to make a warm sauce.

Turn the pudding out onto a platter, then drizzle with the extra sauce and chilled cream to serve. **Serves 4-6**

I like to serve this cake if we celebrate Christmas in July – it's a festive alternative to a traditional pudding. The cranberries add a burst of colour and a lovely tartness.

3 cups (350g) almond meal
2 tsp ground cinnamon
2 tsp baking powder
350g caster sugar
Finely grated zest and juice
    of 1 lemon and 2 oranges
8 eggs
400ml sunflower oil

6 whole cloves
1 cinnamon quill

Cranberry compote
1½ cups (330g) caster sugar
1 cinnamon quill
2 cups (300g) frozen
    cranberries*

Orange & almond cake with cranberry compote

Preheat the oven to 170°C. Grease a 23cm springform cake pan and line the base with baking paper.

Place the almond meal, cinnamon, baking powder, 300g sugar and citrus zest in a large bowl. Make a well in the centre, then add the eggs and oil. Mix well with a wooden spoon until combined. Spread in the prepared pan, then bake for 1 hour or until a skewer inserted in the centre comes out clean (cover loosely with foil if browning too quickly).

Meanwhile, place the citrus juices in a small pan with the cloves, cinnamon and remaining 50g sugar. Stir over low heat to dissolve the sugar, then increase heat to medium and simmer for 3 minutes until slightly reduced. Remove the cake from oven, pierce all over with a skewer, then pour over the syrup. Stand for 1 hour.

For the cranberry compote, place the sugar in a pan with 1 cup (250ml) water and stir over low heat until the sugar dissolves. Add the cinnamon, then simmer for 2 minutes or until thickened slightly. Add the cranberries and cook for 3-4 minutes until the berries have plumped and are starting to burst. Remove the berries with a slotted spoon, then increase the heat to high and simmer the syrup for a further 5 minutes or until thickened. Pour over the berries and allow to cool.

When ready to serve, transfer the cooled cake to a serving platter, then top with the cranberry compote and syrup. **Serves 8.**

* Frozen cranberries are available from supermarkets.

1 cup (170g) pitted dates
1 tsp bicarbonate of soda
90g unsalted butter, softened
125g brown sugar
2 tsp vanilla extract
2 eggs, beaten
175g plain flour
2 tsp baking powder
2 tsp coffee essence*

200g dark chocolate,
    finely chopped
Vanilla or hazelnut ice cream, to serve

Sauce
175g brown sugar
125g unsalted butter
150ml thickened cream
50g dark chocolate, chopped

Sticky mocha pudding with chocolate & toffee sauce

Preheat the oven to 180°C. Grease a 24cm round cake pan and line with baking paper.

Place the dates and soda in a bowl and pour over 175ml boiling water. Set aside for 30 minutes to soften.

Meanwhile, beat the butter, sugar and vanilla together with electric beaters until thick and pale. Add the eggs and beat until well combined.

Place the date mixture and the soaking liquid in a food processor and process until smooth, then add to the cake mixture. Fold in the flour, baking powder, coffee essence and chopped chocolate. Spread into the cake pan, then bake for 45-50 minutes until a skewer inserted in the centre comes out clean. Allow to rest in the pan for 15 minutes before turning out onto a wire rack.

Meanwhile, for the chocolate sauce, place all of the ingredients in a saucepan and stir over low heat for 2-3 minutes until smooth.

Slice cake and serve with ice cream, drizzled with warm chocolate sauce. **Serves 6-8.**
* Coffee essence is available from supermarkets.

3 oranges
1 loaf good-quality sourdough bread (unsliced)
150g unsalted butter, melted
225g Seville orange marmalade*
¼ cup (60ml) Grand Marnier (optional)

3 eggs
100g brown sugar
2 cups (500ml) pure (thin) cream, plus extra to serve
Demerara or raw sugar, to sprinkle
Icing sugar, to dust

Bread & butter pudding with Seville orange marmalade

Preheat the oven to 180°C and grease a 1.5-litre baking dish.

Finely grate the zest of 1 orange, then set aside. Cut away the skin and white pith from all the oranges. Segment the fruit over a bowl to catch the juice, then set the segments and juice aside.

Remove the crust of the sourdough and roughly tear the bread into bite-sized chunks, then place in the baking dish and pour over the melted butter.

Warm the marmalade, reserved orange juice and Grand Marnier, if using, in a small pan over low heat until melted. Pour over the bread, then press in the orange segments.

Place the eggs, brown sugar, cream and zest in a bowl and whisk until combined. Pour over the bread mixture, then stand for 30 minutes to allow the bread to soak up the cream mixture.

Sprinkle with demerara sugar and bake for 40 minutes or until the pudding is golden and the custard is just set. Dust with icing sugar and serve with cream. **Serves 4.**

* Seville orange marmalade is available from gourmet food shops and delis.

Rhubarb & strawberry crumble with custard

1 bunch rhubarb
250g strawberries, halved if large
Grated zest and juice of 1 orange
1 vanilla bean, split, seeds scraped
¼ cup (55g) demerara or raw sugar
300ml creme anglaise
   (see Basics, p 246)

Crumble
2 tbs self-raising flour
2 tbs demerara or raw sugar
¼ cup (25g) walnuts, toasted, chopped
20g chilled unsalted butter

Preheat the oven to 180°C and line a baking tray with baking paper.

Trim the rhubarb, then cut into 8cm pieces. Place the rhubarb in a baking dish in a single layer, then scatter with the strawberries, vanilla pod and seeds, orange zest and juice and the sugar. Cover with foil and bake for 15-20 minutes or until tender but rhubarb is holding its shape.

Meanwhile for the crumble, place the flour in a food processor with the sugar and walnuts. Pulse once or twice to combine, then add the butter and pulse until the mixture comes together in clumps. Spread the crumble mixture onto the lined tray and bake for 15 minutes, stirring once, until golden. Remove from the oven and allow to cool slightly, then break up any large clumps with your fingers.

Pour the creme anglaise into 4 glasses, top with rhubarb and strawberries, then scatter with the crumble mixture and serve. **Serves 4.**

MENUS

fireside supper

130 Hot berry toddies

134 Tartiflette on toast

170 Coconut scones with strawberries and cream

Indian feast

158 Vegetable bhaji salad

148 Goan-style baked fish

178 Orange & almond cake with cranberry compote

Best of British

142 Ham hock terrine with fresh piccalilli

146 Homestyle pies

176 Steamed blueberry pudding

Spice route

136 Asian chicken & coconut soup

150 Pork belly with caramel dressing

174 Moroccan apple pies with rose custard

½ cup (110g) caster sugar
Ice cubes
Juice of 4 lemons

2 cups basil leaves,
  plus extra to serve
Soda water, to serve

Basil lemonade

Place the sugar and ½ cup (125ml) water in a small saucepan and stir over low heat until the sugar dissolves. Increase the heat to medium-high and bring to the boil, then reduce the heat and simmer for 2 minutes or until you have a clear syrup. Remove the sugar syrup from the heat and allow to cool completely.

Half-fill a blender with ice. Add the sugar syrup, lemon juice and basil leaves and blend until smooth. Pass through a sieve, then divide among glasses or bottles and serve with extra ice, topped up with soda water and garnished with basil leaves. **Serves 6.**

This is perfect picnic fare. Pack all of the ingredients into a screw-top jar and keep well chilled until just before serving with crusty bread.

1kg skinless, boneless, red snapper
    fillets, sliced 5mm thick
1 cup (250ml) lime juice,
    plus extra lime wedges to serve
1 red onion, thinly sliced
1 roasted red capsicum*,
    cut into thin strips
3 small red chillies,
    seeds removed, finely chopped
1/2 cup chopped coriander leaves
1 cup (250ml) extra virgin
    olive oil
1/4 cup (60ml) tequila (optional)
Crusty bread, to serve

Snapper ceviche

Combine the fish and lime juice in a bowl (make sure the fish is covered in the lime juice), then cover and marinate in the fridge for 4 hours (the lime juice will gently 'cook' the fish).

Drain off the marinade, then layer the fish in a glass serving bowl or in a sealable jar (if picnicking), alternating layers with the onion, capsicum, chilli and herbs, seasoning well between each layer. Combine the oil and tequila, if using, then pour over the fish. Chill for a further 30 minutes.

Serve with crusty bread, with lime wedges to squeeze over. **Serves 6.**

* Available from delis; or see Basics, p 246.

150g rice vermicelli noodles
½ barbecue chicken
2 tbs sweet chilli sauce
1 tbs lime juice
¼ cup peanuts, chopped
12 x 22cm rice paper sheets*
1 Lebanese cucumber,
  cut into thin matchsticks
2 tbs finely chopped mint
2 tbs finely chopped coriander,
  plus extra leaves to garnish

Dipping sauce
½ cup (110g) caster sugar
¼ cup (60ml) rice vinegar
1 tbs fish sauce
1 tbs sweet chilli sauce
2 small red chillies, finely chopped
2 tbs finely chopped coriander leaves

Chicken rice paper rolls

For the dipping sauce, place the sugar and vinegar in a pan with ¼ cup (60ml) water, then stir over low heat until the sugar dissolves. Cool slightly, then stir in the fish sauce, sweet chilli sauce, chopped chilli and coriander leaves. Set aside until needed.

Place the vermicelli noodles in a bowl and cover with boiling water. Set aside for 5 minutes to soften, then drain and rinse under cold water.

Shred the chicken meat, discarding the skin and bones, then place in a bowl with the sweet chilli sauce, lime juice, peanuts and drained noodles and gently toss to combine.

Fill a large, shallow bowl with hot water. Dip 1 rice paper sheet in the water for 30 seconds or until softened. Remove from the water, then place on a damp tea towel and allow to stand for 30 seconds until opaque and a little drier, but still pliable. Place some of the chicken mixture along the bottom third of the sheet, and top with some of the cucumber, mint and coriander. Fold the bottom edge of the rice paper up over the filling, then fold in the sides and roll up to enclose. Repeat to make 12 rolls.

To serve, garnish with coriander and drizzle with the dipping sauce. **Serves 4.**

* Available from Asian food shops and selected supermarkets.

2 tsp cumin seeds
2 tsp coriander seeds
1/2 cup (100g) dried split green peas
1 1/2 cups (180g) frozen peas, thawed
1 tbs grated lemon zest, plus 1 tbs lemon juice, and wedges to serve
1/2 tsp baking powder
1 tbs plain flour
1/4 tsp chilli powder
2 garlic cloves, roughly chopped
2 tbs chopped flat-leaf parsley leaves
1/3 cup (80ml) sunflower oil, to shallow-fry
4 small pita bread, grilled or warmed

Herby yoghurt
100ml thick Greek-style yoghurt
1 tbs chopped coriander
1 tbs chopped mint, plus extra to serve
Squeeze of lime or lemon juice

Pea felafel with pita & herby yoghurt

Toast the cumin and coriander seeds in a dry frypan over medium heat for 30 seconds or until fragrant. Crush the seeds with the dried split peas in a spice grinder or mortar and pestle to a fine powder, then place in a processor with the thawed peas. Add the lemon zest and juice, baking powder, flour, chilli powder, garlic and parsley, then pulse to form a course paste. Using damp hands, mould the mixture into 12 felafel balls. Chill for 15 minutes or until firm.

Meanwhile, for the herby yoghurt, combine the ingredients in a bowl, then set aside.

Preheat the oven to 170°C. Heat 2cm oil in a non-stick frypan over medium-high heat. In 2 batches, fry the felafel for 4 minutes, turning, until crisp and golden all over. Keep the first batch warm in a low oven while you cook the remaining felafel.

Serve the felafel with the grilled pita, herby yoghurt, lemon wedges and mint leaves.
Makes 12.

750g small squid, cleaned
  (ask your fishmonger to do this)
100g Asian (red) eschalots*,
  thinly sliced
1 lemongrass stem (pale part only),
  thinly sliced
2 long red chillies,
  seeds removed, thinly sliced
2cm piece ginger, cut into matchsticks
3 spring onions, finely shredded
2 tbs chopped mint, plus extra to serve
3 kaffir lime leaves*, finely shredded
Handful Thai basil leaves*

Dressing
2 garlic cloves
2 small red chillies, finely chopped
Juice of 4 limes
1/3 cup (80ml) fish sauce
2 tbs brown sugar

Vietnamese squid salad

For the dressing, place the garlic and chilli in a mortar and pestle and pound to a coarse paste. Place in a bowl, then stir in the lime juice, fish sauce and brown sugar. Set aside.

Cut each squid tube down 1 side and open into a flat piece. Score the inside with a diamond pattern, then cut each piece in half diagonally to form 2 triangles.

Bring a saucepan of salted water to the boil. In 3 batches, cook the squid pieces and tentacles for about 45 seconds until it curls up, making sure to return the water to the boil before cooking the next batch.

Place the hot squid in the bowl of dressing, then add the eschalot, lemongrass, chilli, ginger, spring onion and chopped mint and gently toss to combine. Divide the salad among plates, then garnish with extra mint, kaffir lime and Thai basil leaves. **Serves 6.**
* Available from greengrocers and Asian food shops; substitute regular basil for Thai basil.

3 potatoes (600g total),
  peeled, chopped
600g hot-smoked salmon fillets*
1 tsp fish sauce
1 tsp tomato sauce (ketchup)
1 cup (150g) plain flour,
  seasoned with salt and pepper
3 eggs, lightly beaten
4 cups (200g) panko breadcrumbs*
Sunflower oil, to deep-fry

Green goddess dressing
1 cup (300g) mayonnaise
1 cup (250ml) creme fraiche
  or sour cream
1 tbs white wine vinegar
Juice of ½ lemon
¼ cup each chopped mint and flat-leaf
  parsley, plus extra to garnish
2 tbs each chopped chives and tarragon
1 garlic clove, finely chopped

Salmon croquettes with green goddess dressing

Cook the potatoes in a saucepan of boiling salted water for 8-10 minutes until tender. Drain, then mash until smooth. Transfer to a large bowl.

Flake the salmon, discarding any skin and bones, then add to the bowl of potato with the fish sauce and tomato sauce. Season well with salt and pepper, then mix until well combined. Form into 10 small logs.

Place flour, egg and crumbs in separate bowls. Dip croquettes first in flour, then egg, then in breadcrumbs to coat. Cover and chill for 10 minutes while you make the dressing.

For the dressing, place the ingredients in a food processor and pulse to combine.

Half-fill a deep-fryer or large saucepan with oil and heat to 190°C (a cube of bread will turn golden in 30 seconds when the oil is hot enough). In batches if necessary, deep-fry the croquettes for 3-4 minutes until golden. Drain on paper towel, then serve with the dressing to dip, garnished with extra parsley. **Makes 10.**

* Hot-smoked salmon and panko breadcrumbs are available from supermarkets; substitute regular breadcrumbs for panko.

2 bunches asparagus, ends trimmed
2 cups (300g) fresh podded or frozen broad beans
60g unsalted butter
1 tbs lemon juice
1 tsp white wine vinegar
4 eggs
4 slices sourdough
Olive oil, to brush and drizzle
1 garlic clove, halved
30g shaved pecorino cheese*

Asparagus bruschetta with poached eggs & pecorino

Blanch the asparagus and broad beans in boiling salted water for 2 minutes or until just tender. Drain and refresh in cold water, then remove the outer skins from the broad beans. Melt the butter in a frypan over medium heat. Add the asparagus and broad beans and cook for 1 minute, tossing to coat in the butter. Add the lemon juice and toss to combine, then remove from the heat and set aside.

Meanwhile, bring a shallow pan of water to the boil, add white vinegar, then reduce heat to medium-low. Break eggs into the simmering water and poach for 5 minutes until white is cooked through but yolk is still soft. Remove with a slotted spoon. Keep warm.

Chargrill the bread for 1-2 minutes each side until lightly charred. Rub the toast with the cut side of the garlic and brush with oil. Arrange the vegetables on the toast, sit a poached egg on top, then scatter with cheese and drizzle with oil. Season with sea salt and freshly ground black pepper, then serve. **Serves 4.**

* Pecorino is a hard sheep's milk cheese, available from delis. Substitute parmesan.

70g unsalted butter
2/3 cup (100g) plain flour
2 cups (500ml) milk
7 eggs, separated
1 1/4 cups (100g) grated parmesan, plus 2 tbs extra to sprinkle
1 cup (240g) fresh ricotta

120g soft goat's cheese
1/2 cup (120g) sour cream
1 cup semi-dried tomatoes, drained
1 cup basil leaves
1/2 cup small nicoise olives or other small black olives
Pesto (see Basics, p 246), to serve

Basil, tomato & goat's cheese roulade

Preheat oven to 200°C. Grease a 38cm x 25cm Swiss roll pan and line with baking paper.

Melt butter in a pan over medium-low heat. Add the flour and stir for 1-2 minutes until smooth. Add the milk and whisk gently until thickened. Add the egg yolks one at a time, beating well after each addition, until combined. Remove from the heat and season well.

In a clean bowl, use electric beaters to whisk the eggwhites with a pinch of salt until stiff peaks form. Fold one-third of the eggwhite mixture into the yolk mixture, then use a figure-eight motion to fold in the remaining eggwhites.

Spread the mixture into the prepared pan, sprinkle with 1/3 cup (25g) parmesan and bake for 15 minutes or until the roulade is golden and springs back when gently touched. Turn out onto another sheet of baking paper and allow to cool.

Combine ricotta, goat's cheese, sour cream and remaining parmesan in a bowl. Season well, then spread the cheese mixture over the roulade. Scatter with three-quarters of the tomatoes and a handful of basil. Using the paper as a guide, roll up the roulade from the longest side, finishing seam-side down. Enclose in plastic wrap, then chill for at least 4 hours or overnight to firm.

Preheat the oven to 170°C and line a baking tray with baking paper. Slice the roulade 3-4cm thick. Place the slices on the tray and sprinkle with extra parmesan, then warm through in the oven for 5 minutes or until the cheese just starts to melt. (Alternatively, simply slice and serve the roulade at room temperature.)

Place the roulade slices on a platter, scatter with the remaining tomatoes, olives, and basil leaves, then drizzle with pesto and serve. **Serves 4.**

2 beetroots, trimmed, scrubbed
1 cup (220g) caster sugar
1 onion, thinly sliced
200ml white wine vinegar
200ml thickened cream, whipped to soft peaks
2 tsp lemon juice
¼ tsp dry mustard powder or 1 tsp Dijon mustard
2 tbs horseradish cream
100g baby salad leaves or watercress
1 fennel bulb, thinly sliced
2 x 170g hot-smoked trout fillets*, flaked

Hot-smoked trout salad with horseradish cream

Simmer beetroot in a pan of boiling, salted water until tender (this can take up to 1 hour).

Place all but 1 teaspoon sugar into a saucepan with 400ml water. Stir over low heat until the sugar dissolves. Add the onion and simmer for 3 minutes, then add the vinegar. Peel and slice the beetroot into rounds and add to the onion mixture, then remove from the heat and leave the beetroot to cool in the pickling liquid.

When ready to serve, combine the whipped cream, lemon juice, mustard, horseradish, remaining teaspoon of sugar and some salt and pepper in a bowl.

Strain the beetroot and onion from the pickling mixture and arrange on a plate with the salad leaves, fennel and the flaked salmon. Serve with the horseradish cream. **Serves 4.**
* Hot-smoked trout is from supermarkets.

Chicken pesto pies

The idea of using vol-au-vent cases came from my former assistant Georgina. It's quite ingenious and means no soggy-bottomed pies... thanks Georgie!

40g unsalted butter
1 leek (white part only), thinly sliced
6 button mushrooms, sliced
2 tbs plain flour
¾ cup (185ml) chicken stock
¾ cup (185ml) thickened cream
2 tbs good-quality basil pesto*
 plus extra to serve if desired
3 cups (480g) chopped cooked chicken
6 large, ready-made vol-au-vent cases*
2 sheets frozen puff pastry, thawed
1 egg, lightly beaten
1 tsp nigella seeds* or sesame seeds (optional)
250g vine-ripened cherry tomatoes
1 tbs olive oil

Preheat the oven to 180°C.

Melt the butter in a pan over medium-low heat. Add the leek and cook, stirring, for 5 minutes or until soft. Add the mushroom and cook for a further minute, then add the flour and stir for 1 minute. Gradually stir in the chicken stock, then bring the mixture to simmer. Add the cream and cook for 2-3 minutes, stirring, until thickened. Allow to cool, season, then stir in pesto. Stir the chicken into the sauce.

Using a vol-au-vent as a template, cut 6 lids from the puff pastry sheets. Place the vol-au-vents on a baking tray and fill with the chicken mixture. Brush the edge of the pastry lids with a little water and place on top, pressing the edges to seal. Brush the tops of the pies with the beaten egg and sprinkle with nigella seeds, if using. Bake for 15-20 minutes until golden.

Meanwhile, place the tomatoes on a tray, drizzle with the olive oil and season. Bake in the oven with the pies for 6-8 minutes until the tomatoes are just starting to burst. Serve the pies with the tomatoes and extra pesto, if desired. **Makes 6.**

* Good-quality pesto is from delis; or see Basics, p 246. Vol-au-vent pastries are from the baking section in supermarkets. Nigella seeds are from delis and Asian food shops.

Back in the 1980s when my husband Phil and I worked as a cook and butler team in the UK, coronation chicken was the most popular dish we served. Here I've given it a new look with prawns and a sprinkle of Bombay mix for crunch.

2 tbs sunflower oil
1 large onion, finely chopped
3 tbs (1/4 cup) tikka curry paste*
2 tbs mango chutney, plus extra to serve
1 cup (300g) mayonnaise
150g thick Greek-style yoghurt
500g peeled, cooked prawns (tails intact)
3 spring onions, thinly sliced
3 celery stalks, thinly sliced on an angle, plus celery leaves to garnish
1 mango, thinly sliced
Coriander leaves and Bombay (Bhuja) mix*, to serve

Coronation prawns with Bombay mix

Heat the oil in a frypan over medium heat. Add the onion and cook, stirring, for 2-3 minutes until softened, then add the curry paste and stir for 1 minute or until fragrant. Stir in the mango chutney and 1/3 cup (80ml) water, then remove from the heat and allow to cool.

Place the curry mixture in a food processor or blender with the mayonnaise and two-thirds (100g) of the yoghurt and process until smooth.

Place the prawns, spring onion, celery and mango in a bowl. Add the curry dressing and gently toss to combine. Place on a serving platter, drizzle with the remaining yoghurt, then scatter with Bombay mix, celery leaves and coriander leaves. Serve with extra mango chutney and Bombay mix, if desired. **Serves 4.**

* Tikka curry paste and Bombay (Bhuja) mix are available from selected supermarkets and Indian food shops.

This is a very special surf 'n' turf, where a salad including fennel and exotic dried rose petals add fragrance and flavour to a mixture of pork and prawns.

500g lean pork mince
8 large green prawns, peeled
1 tsp ground cumin
1 red onion, grated
4 garlic cloves, finely chopped
1/2 tsp dried chilli flakes
1/2 bunch coriander, leaves picked
1/4 cup (60ml) olive oil
2 baby fennel bulbs, thinly sliced
6 radishes, thinly sliced
2 tbs dried edible rose petals*
1 tbs lemon juice

Pork & prawn rissoles with fennel & rose petal salad

Place the pork mince, prawn meat, ground cumin, onion, garlic, chilli and most of the coriander into a food processor, reserving some coriander leaves for garnish. Pulse until just combined (don't over-process – you want the mixture to have some texture). Form into 12 patties, then chill for 30 minutes.

Preheat the oven to 180°C.

Heat 1 tablespoon oil in a frypan over medium-high heat. In batches, cook the patties for 2 minutes each side until golden, then place on a baking tray and cook in the oven for 6 minutes or until cooked through.

Combine the fennel, radish and rose petals in a bowl. Add the lemon juice and remaining olive oil, season with salt and pepper, then gently toss to combine.

Divide the patties among plates, then serve with the salad. **Serves 4.**

* Available from gourmet food shops and delis, or at herbies.com.au.

I love kedgeree as it reminds me of leisurely Sunday breakfasts in England. These days, with mango chutney and naan, it makes a great midweek dinner.

300g smoked cod
1 bay leaf
1 tbs olive oil
20g unsalted butter
1 onion, finely chopped
10 fresh curry leaves*
1 cup (200g) basmati rice
1/4 tsp garam masala
8 cardamom pods, lightly crushed
1/2 tsp ground turmeric
2 tsp good-quality mild curry powder
1 1/2 cups fresh or frozen peas
2 tbs roughly chopped flat-leaf coriander, plus extra leaves to garnish
3 spring onions, sliced on an angle
2 hard-boiled eggs, quartered
Fried Asian shallots*, to garnish
Mango chutney, to serve

Simple kedgeree

Cut the cod into large pieces, then place in a pan with the bay leaf and cover with boiling water. Cover and cook over low heat for 8 minutes or until the flesh flakes easily. Remove the fish with a spatula, then strain and reserve the poaching liquid.

Return the cleaned pan to low heat. Add the oil and butter, then add the onion and curry leaves and stir for 2-3 minutes until the onion has softened. Add the rice and stir to coat in the mixture. Add the garam masala, cardamom, turmeric and curry powder, then stir for 30 seconds until fragrant. Add 400ml of the reserved cooking liquid, bring to a simmer and cook for 10 minutes. Add peas and cook for a further 2-3 minutes until the rice and peas are tender, topping up with more cooking liquid if necessary.

Flake the cod into the rice mixture, discarding any skin and bones, then add the coriander and spring onions. Divide among bowls, then garnish with extra coriander, hard-boiled egg and fried shallots. Serve with mango chutney, if desired. **Serves 4.**
* Available from Asian food shops.

I like adding lots of spice to my burgers to make sure they're full of flavour. The tzatziki gives it a cool Mediterranean touch.

1kg lamb mince
1 onion, finely chopped
2 garlic cloves, finely chopped
2 tsp ground cumin
1 tsp ground coriander
1/4 tsp ground cinnamon
1/4 tsp ground allspice
1/2 tsp dried chilli flakes
2 tbs chopped flat-leaf parsley
1 egg

6 sourdough buns, split
2 roasted capsicum*,
    cut into strips

Tzatziki
1 cup (280g) thick Greek-style yoghurt
1 Lebanese cucumber, grated
2 garlic cloves, grated
2 tbs chopped mint,
    plus extra leaves to garnish

Lamb burgers with tzatziki

Place the lamb, onion, garlic, spices, parsley, egg and some salt and pepper in a bowl. Mix with your hands until well combined, then form into 6 patties. Chill for 30 minutes.

For the tzatziki, combine the yoghurt, cucumber, garlic and chopped mint in a bowl. Season, then chill until ready to serve.

Preheat a chargrill pan or barbecue to medium-high heat. Cook the patties for 3-4 minutes each side until cooked through.

Meanwhile, toast the buns, then spread with tzatziki and fill with roast capsicum, lamb patties and extra mint leaves. **Makes 6.**

* Roasted capsicum is available from delis; or see Basics p 246.

2 tbs olive oil
400g chicken breast fillets, thinly sliced
300g marinated chargrilled artichokes, drained, sliced
2 garlic cloves, sliced
1 long red chilli, seeds removed, finely chopped
Grated zest and juice of 2 lemons
400g spaghetti
2 cups wild rocket leaves
½ cup grated parmesan

Lemon chicken & artichoke pasta

Heat the oil in a frypan over medium-high heat. In batches, cook the chicken for 2-3 minutes on each side until golden, adding a little more oil if necessary. Return all of the chicken to the pan with the artichokes, garlic, chilli, lemon zest and juice, then cover and cook over low heat for 5-6 minutes, stirring from time to time, until the chicken is cooked through.

Meanwhile, cook the pasta in a large pan of boiling salted water according to packet instructions. Drain, reserving ¼ cup (60ml) cooking liquid.

Add the pasta and reserved cooking liquid to the pan of chicken and toss over low heat for 1 minute until combined. Season, then add the rocket and toss until just wilted. Serve immediately, topped with grated parmesan. **Serves 4.**

2 tsp ground coriander
2 tsp ground cumin
1 tsp paprika
1/2 tsp ground turmeric
2 garlic cloves, roughly chopped
1 tbs lemon juice
1/4 cup coriander, plus extra to garnish
1/4 cup (60ml) olive oil
4 skinless salmon fillets, pin-boned
2 bunches asparagus, trimmed

Preserved lemon dressing
2 tbs chopped preserved lemon
1/2 cup (150g) whole-egg mayonnaise
2 tbs creme fraiche or sour cream
2 tbs chopped coriander

Moroccan salmon with preserved lemon dressing

Place the spices, garlic, lemon juice, coriander leaves and 1/4 cup (60ml) olive oil in a blender and blend to form a smooth paste. Season well, then coat the fish in the marinade. Cover and marinate in the fridge for 30 minutes.

Meanwhile, for the preserved lemon mayonnaise, combine the ingredients in a bowl, then cover and chill until needed.

Blanch the asparagus in boiling salted water for 2-3 minutes until just tender. Drain, then refresh in cold water. Set aside.

Heat a lightly oiled large frypan or barbecue to medium-low heat. Add the salmon and cook for 4 minutes each side or until golden (but still rare in the centre). Divide the asparagus among serving plates, top with the salmon, then drizzle with the mayonnaise and garnish with extra coriander. **Serves 4.**

- 1 garlic clove, finely chopped
- ¼ tsp paprika
- ½ tsp ground cumin
- ½ tsp dried oregano
- 1 tsp lime juice
- 100ml olive oil
- 2 x 180g scotch fillet or sirloin steaks, halved to give 4 thin steaks
- 3 spring onions, thinly sliced
- 1 bunch coriander, leaves picked
- 2 fresh jalapenos* or other long green chillies, seeds removed, chopped
- 4 vine-ripened tomatoes, chopped
- 2 tbs red wine vinegar
- 4 long crusty bread rolls, split, toasted
- Guacamole (see Basics, p 246), to serve

Mexican steak sandwich

Combine the garlic, paprika, cumin, oregano, lime juice, 1 tablespoon olive oil and some salt and pepper in a bowl. Add the steaks and turn to coat in the mixture. Cover and marinate in the fridge for 2-3 hours.

Place the spring onion, coriander, chilli, tomato, vinegar and remaining olive oil in a bowl. Season well, then stir to combine. Set salsa aside.

Heat a chargrill pan or barbecue on high heat. Cook the steaks for 1 minute each side until charred. Remove and rest, loosely covered, for 2 minutes.

Spread the toasted rolls with guacamole, top with steaks, spoon over salsa, then garnish with coriander leaves and serve with Mexican beer. **Makes 4.**

* Jalapenos are from selected greengrocers and farmers' markets.

I first learnt about 'spoon salads' from Melbourne chef Greg Malouf. The idea is to finely chop your ingredients so they can be served from an elegant spoon.

4 chicken breast fillets
4 tsp harissa*
1/3 cup (80ml) olive oil
5 vine-ripened tomatoes
1 roasted red capsicum*, chopped
2 small red chillies, seeds removed, finely chopped
2 eschalots or 1/2 red onion, finely chopped
1/2 telegraph cucumber, peeled, seeds removed, finely chopped
2 tbs finely chopped flat-leaf parsley
1 tbs finely chopped mint
1 tbs sherry vinegar* or red wine vinegar
Couscous, to serve
Greek-style yoghurt and pita, to serve (optional)

Spicy chicken with spoon salad

Make 3 shallow slashes in each chicken breast. Combine 2 teaspoons harissa and 2 tablespoons olive oil in a bowl, then brush all over the chicken. Cover and marinate in the fridge while you make the salad.

Bring a pan of water to the boil. Cut a cross in the base of each tomato, then place in boiling water for 30 seconds. Plunge into a bowl of iced water. Once they're cool enough to handle, peel the tomatoes, then halve, remove seeds and finely chop. Place the chopped tomato in a bowl with the capsicum, chilli, eschalot, cucumber, parsley, mint, vinegar and remaining harissa and olive oil. Season well with salt and pepper and toss to combine, then place in a sieve set over the bowl and allow to drain for 30 minutes to remove excess liquid.

Preheat a chargrill pan or barbecue to medium-high heat. Cook the chicken for 6-7 minutes each side, turning occasionally, until cooked through. Slice the chicken, then top with the spoon salad and serve with couscous, yoghurt and pita, if desired. **Serves 4.**
* Harissa (a Tunisian chilli paste), roasted capsicum and sherry vinegar are from gourmet food shops and delis; or see Basics, p 246, to roast your own capsicum.

1 2/3 cups (250g) self-raising flour
1/4 cup (60ml) olive oil
1 cup (250ml) good-quality pasta sauce
1 ball of fior di latte* or 2 bocconcini

Toppings
3 slices prosciutto
6 kalamata olives
Fresh basil leaves

Frypan pizza

Sift the flour and 1 teaspoon salt into a bowl. Add 2 tablespoons olive oil and 1/3 cup (80ml) water, then mix with your hands to a soft dough that's not too sticky, adding extra flour if necessary. Dust the workbench with flour, then roll out the pastry into a circle to fit a 26cm frypan.

Preheat a grill to high. Heat 1 tablespoon oil in the frypan over low heat. Add the dough and cook for 3-4 minutes until the underside is crisp and golden. Turn and cook on the other side for 2-3 minutes until golden. Spread with the sauce and top with sliced cheese. Place under the grill and cook for 1-2 minutes until the cheese has melted. Scatter with prosciutto, olives and fresh basil, then serve. **Serves 1-2.**

* Fior di latte is a fresh cow's milk mozzarella, from gourmet food shops and delis.

4 x 4-cutlet racks of lamb,
    French-trimmed
    (ask your butcher to do this)
1 tbs olive oil
100g hazelnuts, roasted, skins removed
1½ cups (100g) fresh breadcrumbs
2 tbs each chopped sage & parsley
6 thyme sprigs, leaves picked
⅓ cup (80ml) thickened cream
2 egg yolks
2 tbs Dijon mustard

Salsa verde
2 cups mint leaves, chopped,
    plus extra leaves to garnish
1 cup flat-leaf parsley,
    leaves chopped
1 tbs salted capers, rinsed, chopped
Juice of 1 lime
100ml olive oil
300g fresh or frozen peas

Spring lamb with pea salsa verde

Remove the lamb from the fridge 30 minutes before you want to cook it to and allow it to come to room temperature – this will ensure the lamb cooks evenly.

Preheat the oven to 200°C.

Heat olive oil in a frypan over medium-high heat. Season the lamb with salt and pepper, then brown the lamb on both sides for 2-3 minutes. Allow to cool.

Meanwhile, place the hazelnuts and breadcrumbs in a food processor and pulse to combine, then add herbs and pulse until chopped. Place in a bowl with the cream, egg yolks and mustard. Season well, then stir to combine – it should be moist enough to stick to the lamb, but not too wet. Adjust with cream or breadcrumbs, if necessary.

Press the breadcrumb mixture evenly onto the skin-side of the lamb. Place the racks on a baking tray, crust-side up, and roast for 12 minutes for pink, or until cooked to your liking. Rest, loosely covered, for 10 minutes.

Meanwhile, make the salsa verde. Combine mint, parsley, capers, lime juice and olive oil in a food processor, pulsing just to combine. Blanch peas in boiling salted water for 2-4 minutes until tender. Drain and refresh in cold water, then add most of the peas to the salsa verde, reserving some to serve. Pulse again until peas are just incorporated. Serve lamb with the salsa verde, garnished with reserved peas and mint leaves. **Serves 4.**

300ml thickened cream
100ml milk
1 vanilla bean, split, seeds scraped
200g white chocolate, chopped
4 egg yolks, beaten
¼ cup (55g) caster sugar

Blueberry compote
¼ cup (55g) caster sugar
200g blueberries
Juice of 1 lime

White chocolate brulee

Place cream, milk and vanilla pod and seeds into a saucepan over medium-low heat and bring to just below boiling point. Place the chocolate in a bowl and pour over the hot cream mixture, then stir for 2 minutes until smooth. Add the egg yolks and return to very low heat, stirring, for 2-3 minutes until slightly thickened. Strain into a jug, then pour into four 200ml glasses or ramekins and chill until set.

Meanwhile, for the blueberry compote, place the sugar and 2 tablespoons water in a pan over low heat and stir until sugar dissolves. Increase the heat to medium and simmer for 1-2 minutes until syrupy. Add blueberries and lime juice and cook for about 2 minutes until they release their juices. Chill in the fridge until ready to serve.

Sprinkle the creams with the caster sugar and use a pastry torch to brulee the tops. Alternatively, heat a grill to high and cook until the sugar melts and caramelises. Serve immediately, topped with the blueberry compote. **Serves 4.**

Just when you thought the cupcake phenomenon was ending, along come ice cream cupcakes!

125g unsalted butter
¾ cup (165g) caster sugar
½ tsp vanilla extract
3 eggs
2 cups (300g) self-raising flour
¼ cup (60ml) milk

12 small scoops of ice cream (such as pistachio, raspberry and vanilla)
Slivered pistachios*, raspberries, chopped white chocolate and berry sauce (see Basics, p 246), to garnish

Ice cream cupcakes

Preheat the oven to 180°C. Line 12 holes in a ⅓-cup (80ml) muffin pan with paper cases.
   Place the butter, sugar, vanilla, eggs, flour and milk in a bowl and beat with electric beaters until smooth. Divide the cake batter among the paper cases and bake for 20-25 minutes until golden and a skewer inserted in the centre comes out clean. Set aside to cool.
   Level the top of each cake by slicing off a small layer. Place cakes on a serving platter, sit a scoop of ice cream on top of each cupcake, and serve immediately with pistachios, raspberries and berry sauce, if desired. **Makes 12.**
* Available from gourmet food shops.

1 qty sweet vanilla pastry
   (see Basics, p 246), or Careme
   sweet shortcrust pastry
200g caster sugar
2 tbs plain flour
400ml buttermilk
3 eggs

50g unsalted butter, softened
Icing sugar, to dust

Passionfruit sauce
½ cup (110g) caster sugar
Seeds and pulp of
   4 passionfruit

Buttermilk tart with passionfruit sauce

Line a 23cm loose-bottomed tart pan with the pastry. Chill for 30 minutes.

Preheat the oven to 180°C. Line the pastry with baking paper and fill with pastry weights or uncooked rice, then blind-bake for 10 minutes. Remove the paper and weights and bake for a further 5 minutes until golden and dry. Allow to cool completely.

Combine sugar, flour, buttermilk, eggs and butter in a bowl, whisking gently to combine. Pour into the cooled tart case, then bake for 45 minutes or until just set.

Meanwhile for the passionfruit sauce, place the sugar and ½ cup (125ml) water in a pan over low heat, stirring to dissolve the sugar. Increase the heat to medium-high and simmer for 5 minutes until syrupy. Stir in the passionfruit, then allow to cool.

Dust the pastry rim with icing sugar, then drizzle the passionfruit sauce over the warm tart and serve immediately. **Serves 8-10.**

* Available from delis and gourmet food shops, visit: caremepastry.com.

This is the ultimate cheesecake. It's super-rich, so serve it in small slices with berries and a drizzle of chocolate sauce.

300g chocolate shortbread biscuits*
70g unsalted butter, melted
750g cream cheese
150g thickened cream
1 vanilla bean, split, seeds scraped
2 eggs, plus 8 egg yolks
240g caster sugar
600ml sour cream
Raspberries or other seasonal berries, and mint leaves, to serve
1 cup (250ml) chocolate sauce (see Basics, p 246), to serve

Classic vanilla cheesecake

Preheat the oven to 160°C. Line a 20cm x 30cm lamington pan with baking paper.

Place the biscuits in a food processor and process to fine crumbs, then add the butter and pulse until just combined. Press biscuit mixture into the base of the prepared pan, then bake for 10 minutes. Allow to cool completely. Reduce the oven to 110°C.

Place the cheese, cream, vanilla seeds, eggs, yolks and 200g sugar in the cleaned processor and process until smooth. Pour the cream mixture over the biscuit base and bake for 1 hour 15 minutes or until just set.

Meanwhile, place the sour cream and remaining 40g sugar in food processor and process until completely smooth. Pour the sour cream mixture over the cheesecake, then return to the oven for a further 15 minutes. The cheesecake will still have a slight wobble. Turn off the heat and allow the cheesecake to cool in the oven with the door ajar. Once cool, chill for 3 hours or overnight until set.

Slice the cheesecake into 12 bars and serve with berries or chocolate sauce, or both.
Serves 12.
* We used Duchy Originals biscuits, available from gourmet food shops. Substitute plain shortbread and 1 tablespoon good-quality (Dutch) cocoa.

1 tbs edible dried lavender flowers*
1 1/3 cups (200g) icing sugar
60g plain flour
1 cup (125g) almond meal
5 eggwhites
180g unsalted butter, melted, cooled

Icing
1 tsp edible dried lavender flowers*
1/4 cup (55g) caster sugar
2/3 cup (100g) icing sugar
Lavender food coloring*
Fresh unsprayed lavender flowers*, to garnish

Lavender friands

Combine the dried lavender flowers and icing sugar, then cover and stand for at least 3 hours, preferably overnight, to infuse.

Preheat the oven to 170°C. Line 9 holes in a friand or patty pan with paper cases.

Place the flowers and icing sugar in a processor and process to a fine powder, then place in a bowl with the flour and almond meal.

In a separate bowl, beat the eggwhites with a fork until frothy, then fold into the dry mixture. Slowly fold in the butter until combined. Divide the mixture among the friand holes, then bake for 10-15 minutes until pale golden.

For the icing, place dried lavender flowers and caster sugar into a spice grinder or mortar and pestle, then grind to a fine powder. Sift the lavender sugar and the icing sugar into a bowl, then stir in 2 tablespoons warm water to make a smooth icing. Add a couple of drops of the food colouring and stir to combine.

To serve, spread icing onto the friands and garnish each with a small lavender flower. **Makes 9.**

* Dried lavender flowers are from delis or herbies.com.au. Lavender food colouring is from cake decorating shops. Fresh lavender flowers are from garden centres.

In South-East Asia, tropical fruits such as pineapple and mango are often livened up with a sprinkle of chilli.

250g golden syrup
1 long red chilli,
    seeds removed, chopped
Finely grated zest of 1 lime
1 mango, peeled, thinly sliced
225g unsalted butter, softened

1 cup (220g) caster sugar
4 eggs
1 tsp vanilla extract
1½ cups (225g) self-raising flour,
    sifted
1-2 tbs milk

Mango & chilli upside-down cakes

Preheat oven to 170°C. Grease the base and sides of a 6-hole (185ml) Texas muffin pan and line with baking paper.

Place golden syrup, chilli and lime zest in a pan and warm gently over medium-low heat for 1-2 minutes. Place 1 tablespoon of the chilli syrup in the base of each muffin hole, reserving the rest to serve. Cover the base with slices of mango, slightly overlapping.

Place the butter and sugar in the bowl of an electric mixer and beat until thick and pale. Add the eggs one at a time, beating well after each addition. Add the vanilla, then fold in the flour. Stir in enough milk to give a soft dropping consistency. Divide the cake batter among the muffin pans, then bake for 20-25 minutes until a skewer inserted in the centre comes out clean. Allow to stand in the pans for 2 minutes before inverting the muffin pan onto a rack to cool completely. (At this stage, I leave the muffin pan over the cakes and sit a chopping board on top to help flatten the base of the cakes so they sit well for presentation.)

When the cakes have cooled, lift off the pan and remove the baking paper. Rewarm the remaining chilli syrup and drizzle over each cake. You can serve the cakes at room temperature or gently rewarmed in a low oven or microwave. **Makes 6.**

The French call it pain perdu, or 'lost bread' – the Yanks call it French toast.

1 cup (250ml) red wine
1/3 cup (75g) caster sugar
400g cherries
1/3 cup (80g) cherry jam
1 egg
1/3 cup (80ml) pure (thin) cream
1 vanilla bean, split,
    seeds scraped
4-8 slices brioche*
30g unsalted butter
Icing sugar, to dust
Vanilla ice cream, to serve

Pain perdu with red wine cherries

Place the wine and 1/4 cup (55g) sugar in a pan over low heat, stirring to dissolve the sugar. Add the cherries to the pan and simmer for 5-6 minutes until softened. Remove the cherries with a slotted spoon and place in a bowl. Add the jam to the pan and cook for a further 3-4 minutes until the sauce is syrupy. Pour the syrup over the cherries, then set aside to cool.

Lightly whisk the egg, cream, vanilla seeds and remaining sugar in a shallow bowl. Dip the brioche slices in the mixture to coat.

Melt the butter in a frypan over medium heat. In batches if necessary, fry the brioche slices for 1 minute on each side until golden. Place the warm brioche on a plate, dust with icing sugar and serve with cherries and ice cream. **Serves 4.**
* Order brioche from bakeries.

MENUS

Spring picnic

192 Snapper ceviche + **196** Chicken rice paper rolls + **238** Lavender friands

Garden party

194 Pea felafel with pita & herby yoghurt + **204** Basil, tomato & goat's cheese roulade + **234** Buttermilk tart with passionfruit sauce

food to share

208 Chicken pesto pies

+

200 Salmon croquettes with green goddess dressing

+

232 Ice cream cupcakes

Dinner for friends

206 Hot-smoked trout salad with horseradish cream

+

228 Spring lamb with pea salsa verde

+

230 White chocolate brulee

BASICS

Aioli

1 cup (250ml) canola oil
50ml lemon-infused extra virgin olive oil*
4 garlic cloves
2 tbs lemon juice
3 egg yolks

Mix the oils in a jug. Place garlic, juice and yolks in a food processor with a pinch of salt, then process to combine. With the motor running, add oil in a slow, steady stream until you have a thick mayonnaise. Season, then cover and chill until needed (up to 4 days). **Makes 1 cup.**
* From gourmet food shops and supermarkets. Substitute regular extra virgin olive oil.

Chocolate pastry

1 1/3 cups (200g) plain flour
2 tbs cocoa powder
40g icing sugar
125g chilled unsalted butter, chopped
1 egg yolk

Whiz the flour, cocoa and sugar in a processor until combined. Add butter and process to fine crumbs. Add yolk and 2 tsp chilled water and process until pastry comes together in a smooth ball. Enclose in plastic wrap. Chill for 30 minutes before rolling out. **Makes a 25cm tart case.**

Chocolate sauce

185g brown sugar
60g unsalted butter
300ml pure (thin) cream
100g dark chocolate (70%), chopped

Place sugar, butter and cream in a pan over medium heat. Bring to the boil, then remove from heat. Add chocolate and stir until melted. Cool before serving. Store in the fridge for up to 5 days. **Makes 1 1/2 cups.**

Chocolate shards

150g good-quality dark, milk or white chocolate

Melt chocolate in a heatproof bowl set over a pan over gently simmering water (don't let the bowl touch the water). Stir until smooth, then pour onto a clean dry surface, metal tray or acrylic board. Use a palette knife to evenly spread to 1mm thick. Leave to set. If the weather is hot, you may need to place it in the freezer for a few minutes. Once set, break into shards.

Alternatively, to make chocolate curls, push the tray of chocolate up against a wall to prevent it moving. Hold a sharp knife or pastry scraper at a 25° angle and push across the surface of the chocolate to form a curl. Chill until ready to use.

Creme anglaise

5 egg yolks
2 cups (500ml) pure (thin) cream
1/4 cup caster sugar
1 vanilla bean, split, seeds scraped

Gently whisk the egg yolks and caster sugar in a bowl until combined. Place the cream and vanilla pod and seeds in a pan over medium heat and bring to just below boiling point. Pour the cream over the egg mixture, whisking gently to combine.

Return the custard mixture to a clean pan and place over very low heat. Stir with a wooden spoon for 5-6 minutes until the mixture thickens and coats the back of the spoon – watch carefully as you don't want to scramble the eggs. (If it does curdle, I've had success with the method used to rescue hollandaise: put everything, except the vanilla bean, in a blender, add an ice cube, then blend well. Keep your fingers crossed.) Strain into a jug. Cover the surface closely with baking paper to prevent a skin forming. Serve warm or chilled. **Makes 2 1/2 cups.**

Dulce de leche

To make this South American milk caramel, remove label from a 400g can sweetened condensed milk, and use a can opener to make 2 small holes in the top of the can. Place the can in a saucepan, opened-side up, and add enough water to almost cover the can. Bring to the boil, then adjust heat to a gentle simmer. Cook for 3 hours, topping up with boiling water as needed. Cool in the water, then open the can and scoop out the caramel.

Flavoured mash

400g Pontiac or desiree potatoes, peeled, chopped
40g unsalted butter
1/3 cup (80ml) pure (thin) cream
3 tsp wasabi paste,
   or 1 tbs truffle-scented oil,
   or 3 tbs grated parmesan,
   or 2 tbs wholegrain mustard

Place the potatoes in a saucepan of cold salted water, bring to the boil and cook for 10 minutes or until cooked through. Drain and pass through a potato ricer or mash well.

Place the butter and cream in a pan over low heat. When butter has melted, add potatoes and flavouring (wasabi paste, truffle oil, parmesan or mustard). Beat with a wooden spoon until smooth and creamy. Season. **Serves 4.**

Guacamole

2 avocadoes, chopped
2 long green chillies, seeds removed, chopped
1/4 cup coriander leaves
1 tbs lime juice
1 tsp ground cumin
1/2 tomato, seeds removed, chopped (optional)

Place the avocado, chilli, coriander, lime juice, cumin and 1/2 teaspoon salt in a processor and process until combined but not smooth – you want to leave some texture in the guacamole. Place in a bowl and stir through the tomato if using. Serve immediately. **Serves 4-6.**

Lemon curd

2 eggs, plus 2 egg yolks
3/4 cup (165g) caster sugar
80g chilled unsalted butter
Grated zest and juice of 2 lemons

Whisk whole eggs, yolks and sugar in a saucepan until smooth, then place pan over a low heat. Add the butter, zest and juice and whisk continuously until thickened. Strain through a sieve into a sterilised jar. Lemon curd keeps, covered, in the fridge for 2 weeks. **Makes 1 1/2 cups.**

Mixed berry sauce

1/2 cup (110g) caster sugar
250g mixed fresh or thawed frozen berries

Place sugar in a pan with 1/4 cup (60ml) of water and stir over medium heat until sugar dissolves. Add berries and cook for 2 minutes, breaking berries up with a spoon. Allow to cool, then puree in a blender. If you prefer a smooth sauce, pass through a sieve. **Makes 1 cup.**

Patatas bravas

1kg pontiac or desiree potatoes, peeled, cut into 2cm cubes
1/3 cup (80ml) dry white wine
1/4 cup (60ml) olive oil
1 onion, finely chopped
2 garlic cloves, chopped
400g can chopped tomatoes
1 tbs tomato paste
1 tsp sweet smoked paprika (pimenton)*
Pinch of sugar
Chopped flat-leaf parsley

Preheat the oven to 190°C.

Place the potato in a saucepan of cold water. Bring to the boil, then cook for 2 minutes until par-boiled. Drain. Place the potato in a baking dish, pour over the white wine, drizzle with 2 tablespoons olive oil and season with sea salt and freshly ground black pepper. Roast for 30-35 minutes until golden.

Meanwhile, heat the remaining olive oil in a pan over medium heat. Add the onion and garlic and cook, stirring, for 2 minutes or until softened. Add the chopped tomatoes, tomato paste, paprika, sugar and some salt and pepper. Bring to a simmer, then reduce the heat to medium and cook for 20-25 minutes, stirring occasionally, until thickened. Cool slightly, then process until smooth. Reheat gently over low heat.

Toss the potatoes in the tomato sauce, then sprinkle with parsley and serve. **Serves 4-6.**
* Smoked paprika is available from gourmet food shops and delis.

Pesto

1 large bunch basil, leaves picked
3 tbs pine nuts, toasted
2 garlic cloves
2/3 cup (50g) freshly grated parmesan
2/3 cup (50g) grated Pecorino Romano*
150-200ml olive oil, plus extra to drizzle

Place basil, nuts, garlic and cheeses in a food processor. Pulse to combine, then gradually add enough oil through the feed tube until you have a luscious green sauce. Transfer to a jar, cover with a thin layer of oil and seal. Chill for up to 1 week – the pesto will darken, but flavour won't be affected. Stir well before using. **Makes 300ml.**
* A hard sheep's milk cheese, from delis. Substitute extra parmesan.

Roasted capsicums

2-3 red capsicums, quartered
Olive oil, to brush

Preheat grill to high. Brush capsicum with oil, then grill for 3-4 minutes until skins blister and blacken. Place capsicum in a bowl, cover with plastic wrap, then stand for 20 minutes or until cool enough to handle. Remove and discard the skin, then slice capsicum into strips, if desired. The capsicum will keep in the fridge, drizzled with a little olive oil, for up to 5 days.

Salsa verde

1/3 cup (80ml) extra virgin olive oil
2 cups flat-leaf parsley leaves
1 cup basil leaves
1/2 cup mint leaves
2 tbs Dijon mustard
2 tbs red wine vinegar
2 tbs salted capers, rinsed
2 anchovy fillets (optional)

Place the ingredients in a blender and blend to form a smooth sauce. Season to taste – remember anchovies and capers are quite salty. Store in the fridge for up to 1 day. **Makes 1 cup.**

Shortcrust pastry

1 2/3 cups (250g) plain flour
180g chilled unsalted butter, chopped

Place the flour and butter in a food processor with a pinch of salt and process until you have fine crumbs. Add 3 tablespoons iced water and process until the mixture comes together and forms a smooth ball. Enclose in plastic wrap and chill for 30 minutes or until ready to use. **Makes a 25cm tart.**

Sweet shortcrust

1 2/3 cups (250g) plain flour
2 tbs icing sugar
1 vanilla bean, split, seeds scraped
180g chilled unsalted butter, chopped
1 egg yolk

Process flour, icing sugar, vanilla seeds and a pinch of salt in a food processor until there are no lumps. Add the butter and process until you have fine crumbs. Add the yolk and 1 tablespoon chilled water, then process until the mixture comes together in a smooth ball. Enclose in plastic wrap, then chill for 1 hour before rolling out. **Makes six 12cm cases or one 25cm case.**

Almond parfait 58
Asian chicken & coconut soup.......136
Asian poached beef on a string 164
Asian-style caprese salad................24
Asparagus bruschetta with
    poached eggs & pecorino 202
Autumn rosti with
    hot-smoked salmon 76
Bagna cauda
    with baby vegetables 80
Baked mushrooms with
    pine nuts and feta........................88
Banana fruit loaf 168
Barbecued prawn cocktails 14
Basil, tomato &
    goat's cheese roulade 204
Basil lemonade 190

beans
    Chicken with butter bean puree
        and crispy chorizo 104
    Fish broth with beans and aioli..132
    Spicy bean soup with
        cumin puris...............................86

beef
    Asian poached beef on a string..164
    Beef carpaccio with
        strawberry vincotto 28
    Beef fillet with beetroot and
        goat's cheese dressing.............34
    Braised beef cheeks with
        salsa verde..............................154
    Crisp stir-fried beef with orange ..98
    Deconstructed lasagne 144

Homestyle pies..........................146
Mexican steak sandwich 222
Steak with mushroom sauce 106

berries
    Beef carpaccio with
        strawberry vincotto 28
    Coconut scones with
        strawberries and cream..........170
    Hibiscus strawberries with
        yoghurt sorbet 62
    Hot berry toddies........................130
    Raspberry &
        white chocolate mousse...........56
    Rhubarb & strawberry crumble
        with custard 184
    Steamed blueberry pudding 176
Bobotie..166
Braised beef cheeks
    with salsa verde 154
Bread & butter pudding with
    Seville orange marmalade.........182
Buttermilk tart with
    passionfruit sauce.....................234

cakes and muffins *see also* desserts
    Coconut scones with strawberries
        and cream...............................170
    Ice cream cupcakes 232
    Lavender friands 238
    Mango & chilli
        upside-down cakes.................240
    Orange & almond cake
        with cranberry compote 178
    Yin-yang chocolate cake 122
Chargrilled swordfish
    with tomatoes and olives 40

cheese
    Asparagus bruschetta with
        poached eggs & pecorino.......202

Baked mushrooms with
    pine nuts and feta.....................88
Basil, tomato &
    goat's cheese roulade 204
Beef fillet with beetroot and
    goat's cheese dressing.............34
Cremets with caramel oranges... 116
Goat's cheese, pear
    & walnut salad..........................78
Harry's Bar sandwiches...............82
Melon & blue cheese salad
    with citrus dressing..................20

cheesecakes *see* chilled desserts
cherries *see* fruit
chicken
    Asian chicken & coconut soup ...136
    Chicken pesto pies 208
    Chicken rice paper rolls.............194
    Chicken tikka
        with minted yoghurt 46
    Chicken with butter bean puree
        and crispy chorizo 104
    Lemon chicken
        & artichoke pasta 218
    Spanish roast chicken
        with quince sauce 152
    Spicy chicken salad
        in wonton cups.........................92
    Spicy chicken with spoon salad..224

chilled desserts
    Almond parfait..............................58
    Cinnamon panna cotta
        with slow-roasted pears.........120
    Classic vanilla cheesecake 236
    'Coconut ice' ice-creams 64
    Hibiscus strawberries
        with yoghurt sorbet 62
    Ice cream cupcakes 232

Limoncello ice cream wedges 60
Mango & coconut trifle................54
Raspberry &
   white chocolate mousse...........56
Vanilla-bean semifreddo with
   pomegranate splash...............124
White chocolate brulee 230

chocolate
Chocolate hazelnut tart..............118
Dulce de leche brownies 114
Raspberry &
   white chocolate mousse...........56
Sticky mocha pudding with
   chocolate and toffee sauce.....180
White chocolate brulee 230
Yin-yang chocolate cake 122

chorizo see sausage
Cinnamon panna cotta
   with slow-roasted pears 120
Classic vanilla cheesecake 236

coconut
Asian chicken & coconut soup ...136
'Coconut ice' ice-creams 64
Coconut scones with
   strawberries and cream.........170
Mango & coconut trifle................54

corn
Crab & corn cakes with
   coriander dipping sauce...........22
Coronation prawns
   with Bombay mix.....................210
Crab & corn cakes with
   coriander dipping sauce...........22
Cremets with caramel oranges.....116
Crisp stir-fried beef with orange.....98

curry
Bobotie 166
Coronation prawns
   with Bombay mix.....................210
Duck & pineapple red curry.......160
Scallops with cauliflower
   skordalia and curry dressing ...84
Deconstructed lasagne.................144

desserts see also cakes and muffins; chilled desserts
Bread & butter pudding with
   Seville orange marmalade.....182
Buttermilk tart with
   passionfruit sauce 234
Lemon curd profiteroles 172
Moroccan apple pies
   with rose custard....................174
Rhubarb & strawberry crumble
   with custard 184
Steamed blueberry pudding 176
Sticky mocha pudding with
   chocolate and toffee sauce.....180
Three-tier brown sugar pavlova...52

dips see sauces, dips and condiments
drinks
Basil lemonade 190
Hot berry toddies......................130
Mulled cider 70
Summer sangria 10
Duck & pineapple red curry...........160
Dulce de leche brownies...............114

fish
Autumn rosti with
   hot-smoked salmon 76
Chargrilled swordfish with
   tomatoes and olives 40
Fish broth with beans and aioli..132
Goan-style baked fish.................148
Hot-smoked salmon salad
   with Thai flavours 32
Hot-smoked trout salad
   with horseradish cream 206
Moroccan salmon with
   preserved lemon dressing......220
Salmon croquettes with
   green goddess dressing 200
Salmon skewers with
   fennel & orange salad 112
Seared sesame tuna
   with soba noodles....................30
Simple kedgeree 214

Smoked salmon crepe cake.........26
Snapper ceviche 192
Tuna tartare with crushed peas...16
Fried squid with
   lime & ginger mayo.....................12

fruit see also berries; lemon; orange
Banana fruit loaf 168
Cinnamon panna cotta
   with slow-roasted pears.........120
Duck & pineapple red curry.......160
Goat's cheese, pear
   & walnut salad..........................78
Mango & chilli
   upside-down cakes.................240
Mango & coconut trifle................54
Melon & blue cheese salad
   with citrus dressing.................20
Moroccan apple pies
   with rose custard....................174
Pain perdu with
   red wine cherries 242
Peach Melba tart.........................50
Pork cutlets with
   peach pan chutney...................42
Spanish roast chicken
   with quince sauce 152
Frypan pizza 226
Garlic prawn pizza bread 36
Goan-style baked fish 148

goat's cheese see cheese
Greek lamb meatball salad 38

ham, bacon and pancetta
Frypan pizza 226
Ham hock terrine
   with fresh piccalilli..................142
Harry's Bar sandwiches............. 82
Onion & bacon tart
   with parmesan cream 138
Sausage saltimbocca 44
Taleggio, pea & pancetta
   pasta bake 96
Harry's Bar sandwiches...................82
Heirloom tomato tarte fine 18

Hibiscus strawberries
   with yoghurt sorbet 62
Homestyle pies 146
Hot and fiery hummus 74
Hot berry toddies 130
Hot-smoked salmon salad
   with Thai flavours 32
Hot-smoked trout salad
   with horseradish cream 206

ice cream *see* chilled desserts
Ice cream cupcakes 232

lamb
   Bobotie 166
   Greek lamb meatball salad 38
   Hot and fiery hummus 74
   Lamb burgers with tzatziki 216
   Lamb cutlets with
      spiced vegetable chips 102
   Lamb & apricot tagine 108
   Spring lamb with salsa verde 228
Lavender friands 238

lemon
   Basil lemonade 190
   Lemon chicken
      & artichoke pasta 218
   Lemon curd profiteroles 172
   Limoncello ice cream wedges 60
   Moroccan salmon with
      preserved lemon dressing......220
Limoncello ice cream wedges 60
Mango & chilli upside-down cakes.. 240
Mango & coconut trifle 54
Melon & blue cheese salad
   with citrus dressing.....................20
Mexican steak sandwich 222
Moroccan apple pies with custard..174
Moroccan pasta 100
Moroccan salmon with
   preserved lemon dressing 220

Mulled cider 70

mushroom
   Baked mushrooms
      with pine nuts and feta 88
   Steak with mushroom sauce 106
Mussels in cider 140

nuts
   Almond parfait 58
   Baked mushrooms
      with pine nuts and feta 88
   Chocolate hazelnut tart..............118
   Goat's cheese, pear
      & walnut salad.........................78
   Orange & almond cake
      with cranberry compote 178
   Onion & bacon tart.......................138

orange
   Bread & butter pudding with
      Seville orange marmalade 182
   Cremets with caramel oranges ..116
   Crisp stir-fried beef with orange..98
   Orange & almond cake
      with cranberry compote 178
   Salmon skewers with fennel
      & orange salad 112
Pain perdu with red wine cherries..242

pasta
   Deconstructed lasagne 144
   Lemon chicken
      & artichoke pasta 218
   Moroccan pasta 100
   Taleggio, pea & pancetta
      pasta bake 96

pavlova
   Three-tier brown sugar pavlova...52
Peach melba tart 50

pear
   Cinnamon panna cotta
      with slow-roasted pears.........120

   Goat's cheese, pear
      & walnut salad.........................78

peas
   Pea felafel with herby yoghurt ...196
   Spring lamb with
      pea salsa verde......................228
   Taleggio, pea & pancetta
      pasta bake 96
   Tuna tartare with crushed peas ..16

pies and pastries *see also* pizzas; tarts
   Chicken pesto pies 208
   Homestyle pies..........................146
   Moroccan apple pies
      with rose custard 174
Pimientos de Padron 72

pizzas
   Frypan pizza 226
   Garlic prawn pizza bread 36

pork
   Pork & olive stew 162
   Pork & prawn rissoles with
      fennel & rose petal salad 212
   Pork belly with
      caramel dressing...................150
   Pork cutlets with peach chutney..42
   Roast pork with
      Marsala & fig sauce............... 110
   Sticky pork ribs 48
   Vietnamese pork baguette...........90

potatoes
   Patatas bravas.......................... 248
   Tartiflette on toast..................... 134

prawns *see* seafood
puddings *see* desserts
Pumpkin & leek tart
   with pan-fried mushrooms 94
Raspberry &
   white chocolate mousse 56
Rhubarb & strawberry crumble
   with custard...............................184
Roast pork with Marsala sauce 110

salads
   Asian-style caprese salad............24

Greek lamb meatball salad...........38
Hot-smoked salmon salad
   with Thai flavours......................32
Hot-smoked trout salad
   with horseradish cream..........206
Melon & blue cheese salad
   with citrus dressing...................20
Salmon skewers with
   fennel & orange salad.............112
Spicy chicken salad
   in wonton cups.........................92
Spicy chicken with spoon salad..224
Vegetable bhaji salad 158
Vietnamese squid salad 198

salmon see **fish**

sandwiches, rolls and toast
   Asparagus bruschetta with
      poached eggs & pecorino.......202
   Chicken rice paper rolls.............194
   Harry's Bar sandwiches...............82
   Lamb burgers with tzatziki 216
   Mexican steak sandwich 222
   Pain perdu with
      red wine cherries 242
   Tartiflette on toast......................134
   Vietnamese pork baguette...........90

sauces, dips and condiments
   Bagna cauda with
      baby vegetables.......................80
   Ham hock terrine with piccalilli..142
   Hot and fiery hummus 74
   Lamb burgers with tzatziki 216
   Pea felafel with herby yoghurt...196
   Pork belly with
      caramel dressing 150
   Pork cutlets with
      peach pan chutney...................42
   Roast pork with
      Marsala & fig sauce............... 110
   Salmon croquettes with green
      goddess dressing....................200
   Spanish roast chicken
      with quince sauce 152

sausage
   Chicken with butter bean puree
      and crispy chorizo 104
   Chorizo carbonara......................156
   Sausage saltimbocca 44
   Scallops with cauliflower
      skordalia and curry dressing 84

seafood
   Barbecued prawn cocktails 14
   Coronation prawns
      with Bombay mix 210
   Crab & corn cakes with
      coriander dipping sauce...........22
   Fried squid with lime
      & ginger mayo 12
   Garlic prawn pizza bread 36
   Mussels in cider 140
   Pork & prawn rissoles with
      fennel & rose petal salad 212
   Scallops with cauliflower
      skordalia and curry dressing ...84
   Vietnamese squid salad 198
   Seared sesame tuna with soba....... 30
   Simple kedgeree 214
   Smoked salmon crepe cake............26
   Snapper ceviche............................192

soup, stews and broths
   Asian chicken & coconut soup ...136
   Fish broth with beans and aioli..132
   Pork & olive stew 162
   Spicy bean soup with cumin puris ..86
   Spanish roast chicken
      with quince sauce......................152
   Spicy bean soup with cumin puris.. 86
   Spicy chicken salad in wonton cups..92
   Spicy chicken with spoon salad 224
   Spring lamb with pea salsa verde..228

squid see **seafood**
   Steak with wild mushroom sauce...106
   Steamed blueberry pudding 176
   Sticky mocha pudding with
      chocolate & toffee sauce............180
   Sticky pork ribs 48

strawberries see **berries**
   Summer sangria 10
   Tartiflette on toast.........................134

tarts see also **pies and pastries**
   Buttermilk tart with
      passionfruit sauce 234
   Chocolate hazelnut tart..............118
   Heirloom tomato tarte fine 18
   Onion & bacon tart
      with parmesan cream 138
   Peach Melba tart 50
   Pumpkin & leek tart with
      pan-fried mushrooms 94
   Three-tier brown sugar pavlova 52

tomato
   Basil, tomato &
      goat's cheese roulade 204
   Chargrilled swordfish with
      tomatoes and olives 40
   Heirloom tomato tarte fine 18

vanilla
   Classic vanilla cheesecake 236
   Vanilla-bean semifreddo with
      pomegranate splash...............124

vegetables
   Autumn rosti with
      hot-smoked salmon 76
   Bagna cauda with
      baby vegetables 80
   Lamb cutlets with
      spiced vegetable chips 102
   Vegetable bhaji salad 158
   Vietnamese pork baguette...........90
   Vietnamese squid salad................198
   White chocolate brulee 230
   Yin-yang chocolate cake 122

yoghurt
   Chicken tikka with
      minted yoghurt 46
   Hibiscus strawberries
      with yoghurt sorbet 62
   Pea felafel with
      herby yoghurt 19

Thanks

A COOKBOOK IS always about so much more than simply the recipes that go into it. From the early planning stages to sourcing the props, shopping for ingredients, setting up the perfect shot and then making sure it all comes together on time, there are so many different people involved in the process.

Fortunately for me, my team has been amazing. To photographer Brett Stevens, a million thankyous as always for your unique and beautiful work. Thanks also to stylist David Morgan, who is such a talent and has given the book a special quality and feel.

It's been a pleasure shooting in our wonderful new studio – thanks to Elizabeth Hachem and Nigel Lough for their hard work.

To Jess Brook and Phoebe Wood, my wonderful food team, who did the long slog with me in the kitchen without complaint.

A heartfelt thanks to Sarah Lewis, the project editor, who has done such a great job in holding things together in her usual efficient and effortless way. To Shannon Keogh, who put so much creative energy and enthusiasm into the design of the book – I really appreciate the extra effort you've put in. Thanks also to a returning team member, Michael Shafran for his great editing work.

A huge thanks to Danielle Oppermann, our managing editor (still my rock!) and our talented creative director, Scott Cassidy, who has once again helped to make a beautiful book that we can all be proud of.

Meanwhile, as the show goes on in the *delicious.* office, the team has been wonderfully supportive and creative, and have continued to do what they do so well in producing our fabulous magazine every month. Senior designer Simon Martin and the editorial team of Alison Pickel, Kate Skinner and Jacqui Gal Cohen – big hugs to you all.

This cookbook wouldn't have been possible without Trudi Jenkins, our editor-in-chief, who continues to offer her constant support, encouragement and advice after almost 10 years working together on *delicious*.